FROM THE RIVERBANK TO MIDDLE EARTH AND BEYOND

PAT SHIRLEY

Order this book online at www.trafford.com
or email orders@trafford.com

Most Trafford titles are also available at major online book retailers.

Printed in the United States of America.

ISBN: 978-1-4669-7457-9 (sc)
ISBN: 978-1-4669-7456-2 (e)

Library of Congress Control Number: 2012924148

Trafford rev. 07/20/2013

 www.trafford.com

North America & international
toll-free: 1 888 232 4444 (USA & Canada)
fax: 812 355 4082

For my mother, who read *The Wind in the Willows* and Felix Salten's *Bambi* in their complete, original, "not just for children" form many times to me when I was six to ten and enjoyed them each time as much as I did.

And for my aunts and uncles, in whom I was more fortunate than Kenneth Grahame believed he was in his.

I

Introduction

I received Kenneth Grahame's *The Wind in the Willows* as a present on my seventh birthday. My mother probably read it to me at least fifty times in the next few years. A cousin who was in college studying to be an English teacher suggested it as a gift for me. One of her teachers finished out class time reading aloud from her favorite books, of which *The Wind in the Willows* was one. I later learned that my cousin's teacher continued to read it every other year for the rest of her life. Her devotion to it and the comment of an adult fictional character on TV that *The Wind in the Willows* was her favorite book convinced me that it isn't just for children and that I could go back to it. I now read it once a year.

Not long before I rediscovered *The Wind in the Willows*, J.R.R. Tolkien became very popular. I read and loved *The Lord of the Rings*. Probably because reading the three books is a considerable undertaking, I had not re-read it when publicity for the first of the live-action movies revived an interest I had not considered lost. I patiently waited to see the movie and judge it for itself before re-reading *The Fellowship of the Ring*. I enjoyed the movie very much and reading the books again even more. What impressed me most in acquainting myself again with the trilogy was how many images and phrases reminded me of *The Wind in the Willows*, a book with which I was particularly familiar by then from my yearly reading. I set out to find if Tolkien had ever said that Grahame influenced him or if a scholar had ever suggested it. Similarities could be due to the fact that they were similar men with similar backgrounds, living in essentially the same culture, time, and place. Influence could be unconscious. How many people read *The Wind in the Willows* when very young or had it read to them and do not remember the source of the influence it makes on their lives, values, and writing. I found only Brian Jacques listing Grahame among the writers who influenced him. Even Jacques places Grahame last of eight influences, though *The Wind in the Willows* must have had a very direct influence on his creating the animals in the *Redwall* series.

However, Tolkien does state in the first note to his essay "On fairy Stories" that he read and much admired *The Wind in the Willows*.[2] Douglas A. Anderson points out in his *Tales Before Tolkien* that Tolkien considered *The Wind in the Willows* an excellent book. I sincerely thank Anderson for sharing the source of his information with me and bringing my search for a direct link between the two writers to a successful conclusion.

Perhaps Tolkien relegated Grahame's influence to an endnote because he assumed it to be known that *The Wind in the Willows* is the bedrock of modern fantasy. As A.A. Milne said:

> One does not argue about *The Wind in the Willows*. The young man gives it to the girl with whom he is in love, and, if she does not like it, asks her to return his letters. The older man tries it on his nephew and alters his will accordingly. The book is a test of character. We can't criticize it, because it is

criticizing us. But I give you one word of warning. When you sit down to it, don't be so ridiculous as to suppose that you are sitting in judgment on my taste, or on the art of Kenneth Grahame. You are merely sitting in judgment on yourself. You may be worthy, I don't know. But it is you who are on trial.[4]

Tolkien points out in that same first note to *On Fairy Stories* that it is strange that, as he held this opinion of *The Wind in the Willows*, it was Milne who, through his play *Toad of Toad Hall*, relegated the book to the realm of children's literature for most people. Tolkien believed that Milne should not have dramatized the book.[5] However, Grahame is said to have approved making it a play and making it a play for children. If Milne made the River more shallow, he increased its length and breadth. He greatly increased its fame and popularity. Perhaps he and Grahame sensed that if enough people were introduced to the story and were interested, inspired, or curious enough to go on to read Grahame's complete book, some of them would see the truth in the River's depth.

Apparently Tolkien greatly admired *The Wind in the Willows* and wanted to go where it would take him and plunge the River's depth. Much of the early draft of the story had been written as letters to Grahame's son. These letters were published by Grahame's widow after Grahame died. Tolkien wrote his son Christopher July 31-August 1, 1944 that he must obtain a copy of these letters.[6]

I formed an early impression that *The Lord of the Rings* is similar to *The Wind in the Willows* but darker and deeper. By the time I had finished Tolkien's trilogy for the second time and read *The Wind in the Willows* yet again, I reversed this opinion. Peter Hunt calls *The Wind in the Willows* many-layered and allusive.[7] It has been said that one should read it every ten years and that we will find a different book with each reading. However, the story we read each time seems straightforward enough. It seems perfectly natural for toads to drive motorcars and live in mansions and for rats and moles to act and dress like proper Edwardian gentlemen. If we are being presented with humans, their animal personas seem natural as well. In his biography of Grahame, Peter Green says that characterization was Kenneth Grahame's highest gift.[8] His true and unique genius was in bringing together Edwardian society and the timeless world of nature. Tolkien's purpose was to create a new world or re-create an old, forgotten middle time that might have been. Both men created lasting works of genius.

In his ability to combine worlds, Grahame's reality is limitless. Converging worlds have no boundaries. There are depths in Grahame's River that we will never fathom. There are whispers in the wind that we will never clearly hear. Grahame was a successful but tragic man. Ironically, he could not draw his own character or integrate his own personality. Part Mole, part Rat, part Badger, part Otter, part Toad, we cannot understand him. He did not understand himself.

Tolkien seems to have been a basically happy and straightforward man. He worked backwards logically to create his imagined but straightforward world. Middle Earth is intricate and complex but well-ordered. At least on a surface level, it is drawn on simple moral and philosophical lines. In the late 1960's and at the turn of the millennium, *The Lord of the Rings* was very popular. People were expecting the great battle between good and evil in which the world as we knew it would end. Tolkien's trilogy was seen as depicting such a battle. These were times of rapid change in which the world as we knew it was actually ending, great battle or no, as certainly as

Middle Earth gave way to the Age of Man. Tolkien did not much like modernity and rapid change. Yet he accepted that his world was ending just as Treebeard and the elves did. In *Author of the Century*, Shippey asks if one can be sad and happy at the same time. He finds a definition of courage in this acceptance of the way things are and that sacrifices must be made for the sake of preservation.[9] This is typical of Tolkien's thinking. He brought his friend C.S. Lewis back to Christianity by relating Lewis's respect for sacrifice in the old myths to the Christian faith.

However, Tolkien was less clear in his feelings about evil and war than it might seem at first reading. One can see the questions, "How evil is Evil?" and "Is war an acceptable answer?" nagging at his mind. Tolkien created some unattractive characters, seemingly devoid of saving grace. However, they are not truly evil. The true evil is power itself. Tolkien took power very seriously. Grahame satirized it. Tolkien would have agreed with Henry Thoreau that power corrupts and absolute power corrupts absolutely. Tolkien's "evil" characters have been eaten away by power or the lust for power. Nothing is evil in the beginning.[10]

Shippey sees Smeagol/Gollum as having once been a hobbit, deformed by his long obsession with the Ring. Shippey believes that even Gollum might have been "saved" had Sam not misunderstood and rejected his attempt to show loyalty and affection for Frodo.[11] That he will return to treachery in the end is not a foregone conclusion.

Tolkien's human Boromir is a truly sympathetic character. He is flawed but well-intentioned and certainly not evil. He has the human faults of greed, selfishness, and ego. He wants to use the power of the Ring to help his people. He could have destroyed the entire enterprise by his conceit that evil in the proper hands can bring about good. Tolkien knew first-hand that war comes of such conceit. His service in WWI had to have influenced his writing. Sam followed Frodo as servants followed masters to the war. Sam's view of war in *The Two Towers* must surely have come from Tolkien's own memory.

> For a moment he caught a glimpse of swarthy men in red running down the slope some way off with green-clad warriors leaping after them, hewing them down as they fled. Arrows were thick in the air. Then suddenly straight over the rim of their sheltering bank, a man fell, crashing through the slender trees, nearly on top of them. He came to rest in the fern a few feet away, face downward, green arrow-feathers sticking from his neck below a golden collar. His scarlet robes were tattered, his corslet of overlapping brazen plates was rent and hewn, his black plaits of hair braided with gold were drenched with blood. His brown hand still clutched the hilt of a broken sword.
>
> It was Sam's first view of a battle of Men against Men, and he did not like it much. He was glad he could not see the dead man's face. He wondered what the dead man's name was and where he came from; and if he was really evil at heart, or what lies and threats had led him on the long march from his home; and if he would really rather have stayed there in peace.[12]

Tolkien must have felt pity for German soldiers that he fought. It is not difficult to imagine him foregoing a chance to kill.

Gandalf's speech to Frodo on Bilbo's pity for Gollum compares with Shakespeare's "quality of mercy" and the Bible's "judge not". It recurs in the trilogy and is a major theme.

> What a pity Bilbo did not stab the vile creature when he had the chance!
>
> Pity? It was pity stayed his hand. Pity and mercy: not to strike without need.
>
> I do not feel any pity for Gollum. He deserves death.
>
> Deserves death! I daresay he does. Many that live deserve death. And some die that deserve life. Can you give that to them? Then be not too eager to deal out death in the name of justice, fearing for your own safety. Even the wise cannot see all ends.[13]

The National Geographic Explorer television documentary *Lord of the Rings, Beyond the Movie* views the trilogy as an anti-war statement that depicts the horrors of war. *The Hobbit* had also expressed a preference for peace.

> Goblins have probably invented many machines that have since troubled the world, especially devices for killing large numbers of people at once, but had not then advanced (as it is called) so far.[14]

I did not set out to retell the stories but to look for similarities in the lives and work of the authors. I wanted to explore the sources of their inspiration and world-view and to look for possible influence they may have had on some other writers of modern fantasy. I also wanted to ask why these books have continued to have such timeless and ageless appeal.

In exploring the two men's attitude to such universal issues as war and peace, I found that although both seem to have accepted war as sometimes necessary or simply a recurring fact of life in the world Tolkien preferred the peaceful life of the Shire to the World War battlefields that influenced the rest of his life and his writing. Like many other idealistic young Englishmen of his generation, he went to war in search of glory and an easy victory and was disillusioned by misery, doubt, and degradation. Frodo found little glory in doing what needed to be done. There was actually more glory in the retaking of Toad Hall than in Frodo's entire saga.

There is little glory in Tolkien's depiction of war, and Frodo had little honor in his own country when he came home.[15] He did come home but could be considered sacrificed in a nearly unnoticed way.[16] Tolkien's imagery was often subtle and came from his Catholic faith as well as from the old Norse myths. Sam was tempted much as Jesus was.[17]

Grahame much preferred the quiet life of the Riverbank to the Wide World, into which he had to make frequent excursions to perform his duties as a banker, work at which he was quite good, health and inclination permitting. He might have been an even better banker if he hadn't so much preferred excursions across the downs and the company of his Riverbank friends. Unlike Frodo and company, Mole, Rat, Badger, and Toad became legends in their own time and were treated with great respect ever after their exploit that recaptured Toad Hall. They gained fame and glory without leaving their own home ground. In spite of necessary time spent in London, in spirit, Grahame spent his life on the Riverbank. To a greater extent than Tolkien, he lived apart from the Wide World.

Also unlike Tolkien, Grahame did not use sweeping themes or such firm divisions as good and evil. Toad could be very bad but was essentially good-hearted on the rare occasions when the welfare of someone other than himself occurred to him. Even the stoats and weasels lacked only civilization and could learn to behave in acceptable ways. Perhaps the moral was that Grahame's son Alastair could do the same. Grahame had begun telling these stories to his son on Alastair's fourth birthday in May 1904.[18] It is ironic that a writer who loved nature and admitted a preference for small wild animals over people equated goodness with civilization or at least socialization in his animal characters. Of course, some of Grahame's irony was ironic or satiric humor. The attempts of Toad's friends to impose their morals and values forcibly upon him may in part be satiric of society's attempts to forcibly impose values and legislate morality. Beyond Toad's socially unacceptable behavior are the Wild Wooders. Grahame had to have known that the Wild Wooders had a supportable point of view. Jan Needle's book *Wild Wood* is the story from the point of view of the stoats and weasels, being to *The Wind in the Willows* what John Gardner's *Grendel* is to *Beowulf.*

Grahame scholar Peter Green calls it Grahame's affectation to understand the speech of animals.[19] This is rather presumptuous of Green, as many people from horse whisperers to veterinarians to pet owners claim to communicate with animals. Ability or affectation, giving speech to his Edwardian animals must have seemed natural to Grahame. Tolkien created complex and logical languages working backwards from those that would have come after them. He created complete species of creatures. However, among his animals, only his birds can talk. As Grahame understood the speech of small, wild animals, the people of Dale understood Tolkien's thrush.[20] They depicted animals differently, but many similarities can be found in the lives and work of Grahame and Tolkien. Peter Hunt mentions Tolkien when writing about Grahame, perhaps recognizing an influence that Tolkien mentioned less often than one might expect. Tolkien's friend C. S. (Jack) Lewis claimed Grahame among his own influences. Hunt points this influence on Lewis out in *A Fragmented Arcadia*.[21] Lewis wrote of Grahame and Badger in *Three Ways of Writing for Children*.[22] Lewis also wrote of badgers in the first of his *Chronicles of Narnia, The Lion, the Witch, and the Wardrobe*, in which book he also personified trees, as did Tolkien. Lewis wrote of the souls of trees, good and bad trees, and trees that take sides. Tolkien's trees go to war. When Grahame's Mole entered the Wild Wood alone in search of Badger and became lost and over taken by night, he saw trees as malicious being coming after him.

Tolkien biographer Carpenter believed that Tolkien may have resented Lewis for drawing on his ideas to write a simpler and less time and effort intensive tale in *The Chronicles of Narnia*.[23] If so he may have been disinclined to emphasize the influence that Grahame had on his writing. At least on the surface, *The Wind in the Willows* was also a simpler tale. *The Lord of the Rings* had become serious and grand, and Grahame was not a bone fide, credentialed scholar.

There must have been many informal comparisons to *The Wind in the Willows* when Tolkien's simpler tale *The Hobbit* was published, as the children's librarian at the NY Public Library considered such comparisons to be unfair because of *The Hobbit's* firm foundations in myths and legends such as *Beowulf*.[24]

I do not expect readers of this book to be scholars in the sense that Tolkien was. I do expect that readers will previously have read *The Wind in the Willows, The Hobbit* and *The Lord of the Rings*, as I do not explain who the characters are or the situations in which we find them.

The Writers and
Their World

J.R.R. Tolkien (1892-1973) had to have been in some degree familiar with the life and work of Kenneth Grahame (1859-1932). He was sixteen when *The Wind of the Willows* was published and would not have read it as a child, although he may well have read it to his children. Both men had connections to Oxford and spent part of their lives in that part of England. Grahame attended Oxford's preparatory school and was greatly disappointed when his relatives declined to spend the money to send him to the university. His son Alastair did attend Oxford University. Tolkien also attended, as a scholarship student, and returned as a professor in 1925, just five years after Alastair's death there. Surely there were still whispered stories of Alastair's tragic end.

Neither Grahame nor Tolkien grew up in a traditional home. Grahame's mother died of scarlet fever when he was five. His alcoholic father turned the raising of the children over to their maternal relatives. Tolkien's father died when he was four and his mother when he was twelve. Both Tolkien and Grahame were "poor relation", although Tolkien was more so. His mother might have received help from her own family and her late husband's if she

13

had not converted to Catholicism, a religion of which both families disapproved. A different sort of son might have considered his mother foolish and resented their poverty. Tolkien considered her to be a heroine, a saint, and a martyr. He remained loyal to both her memory and the Catholic Church all of his life. He had no trouble reconciling his Christian faith with the old myths he loved and the ones he created.

It was out of his tension and conflict that Grahame's genius came. He lived on the edge of Society through his family, his position at the bank, and the literary circle in which he was included. He aspired to a higher standing. At the same time, he was an (almost) outside observer and saw it all as absurd. He could laugh at what he wanted and laugh at himself for wanting it. It gave his work the perfect blend of sympathy and satire. He was a reserved but generally sympathetic man. He was a sad man saved by humor.

Grahame's satire is often missed, most often by those who take too seriously his writing, or lack thereof, about women. Both he and Tolkien lived in a male-oriented world. Women are more prominent in Tolkien's work, but male fellowship forms the basis of his books. He had a good marriage but probably spent more time talking with his male friends than with his wife. Tolkien and his friend C.S. Lewis were part of a small group of Oxford teachers who called themselves the Inklings and met to discuss and translate the old Norse myths. Tolkien said that at Oxford he sat late at night smoking and talking to friends in front of the fire.[1] He was referring to his student days, but he could have said the same of himself as a professor. Of course, this was a favorite pastime of Hobbits and Riverbankers as well.

Tolkien worked on translations with women who were or had been his students, but he related to them as scholars, not women, and the camaraderie of the Inklings was no doubt not there. The social boundaries that segregated men and women were breaking down in Tolkien's time, but tradition remained strong at Oxford. In Grahame's day, the separation was even more pronounced.

Grahame retired early from the bank, four months before *Wind in the Willows* was published in 1908, mostly because of poor health. There was also the consideration that he did not get on well with the bank's new efficiency-minded governor, who had been appointed the year before. Aside from often being ill, Grahame tended to put in short days and take long vacations, country air and nature walks being his health remedies of choice. He was always the proper businessman at work, but even his already published writing must have been rather an embarrassment by not conveying the image the bank wanted from its Secretary. Now it was rumored that he had written about a mole and a rat in the guise of gentlemen (or gentlemen in the guise of a mole and a rat), probably in part on bank time.

Grahame more likely regretted the time he spent being a proper banker than the time he spent writing and walking in the country. With Henry David Thoreau in *Walden*, he would have said that if he repented of anything it would very likely be his good behavior. For whatever combination of reasons he left. Grahame was well gone from The Bank of England. He had more basic conflicts, however, than those the business world exacerbated. He saw himself as a rebel against his society's constrictions but continued to act with conformity and respectability. He had both liberal and conservative tendencies. He accepted the class structure from which he benefited and believed he should benefit more. Yet, while living in London, he did volunteer social work in the East End. Of course, this may not have been an entirely liberal impulse. He may have felt about East End immigrants as Rat and Mole felt about Wild Wooders and about Toad. "If they are going to live among us, we must socialize them and civilize them. They must behave properly, as we do."

When he was nine, Tolkien and the family lived beside a railroad and coal yard. His fascination with language grew from his attraction to the Welsh words painted on the cars. He retained a hatred of railroads along with a love for language, although he tolerated the passion his sons had for trains as children.

Grahame's childhood living conditions were not as poor as Tolkien's, but, although both men were apparently pleasant and convivial and had good friends, Grahame always saw himself as living on the fringe of his mother's family and of society, the poor relation or casual acquaintance of everyone.

Both men had banking connections. In lieu of a university education, Grahame's uncle recommended him for a clerkship in the Bank of England. He rose to be the Bank's youngest Secretary. Tolkien's father was a banker and conceivably could have met Grahame while job hunting in the late 1880's.

Tolkien's career as a professor did not directly conflict with his writing, although he sometimes resented that his more mundane duties at Oxford took time away from the creation of Middle Earth. Grahame's duties at the bank conflicted seriously with not only his writing but with his values and beliefs. A fragmented and conflicted personality was forged into definite divisions. Like Tolkien, Grahame hated railroads. To both men they were dirty and noisy and marred the natural beauty of the countryside. The Bank of England financed railroad construction. Grahame had a successful career in banking, but the stress of such an uncongenial job must have put further strain on his fragile health. He had had problems with bronchitis and emphysema and had not really been well since age five, when he had contracted the scarlet fever that killed his mother.

Grahame may have had little interest in sex, but there is no reason to think, as Peter Hunt does, that he was a misogynist or more of an anti-feminist than most men of his day. People must be considered in the context of their time. Hunt cites the lack of proper names for women.[2] Neither do the male characters in *Wind in the Willows* have proper names. Hunt sees Washerwoman and Bargewoman as being presented in a negative way. Washerwoman, like her niece the jailer's daughter, is actually kind and brave. Of course, Grahame, when the jailer's daughter tells Toad that she has an aunt who is a washerwoman, remembers his childhood among uncles and aunts and can't resist giving Toad the line:

> There, there, never mind; think no more about it. *I* have several aunts who *ought* to be washerwomen.[3]

It is Toad as Washerwoman who is ridiculous, not Washerwoman herself. Bargewoman discovers Toad's true identity and throws him overboard. Toad is made the fool, not Bargewoman.

Hunt says that women looked at Toad and saw a toad, that they ruined the story by seeing the wrong thing. "If this is wisdom in a sense, it is wisdom the male world fears and does not want to acknowledge."[4]

Perhaps it is satire. Maybe it's a joke. Perhaps those who say Grahame hated women should lighten up. It's a long leap from "seeing the wrong thing" to misogyny. If it is satire, are women or society's attitude toward women being satirized?

I am a woman and a moderate feminist. More than half of *The Wind in the Willows* devotees that I know of are women. One wonders how an anti-feminist and misogynist inspired so much admiration from women.

Grahame corresponded with women about his books and had a very congenial relationship with his cousin Annie. Peter Green assumes presumptuously that she hoped to marry him.[5] There is no evidence for this, although she probably missed his companionship when he married. She never married, but perhaps she was not the marrying kind. He was not the marrying kind and should not have married either. If marry he must, he would have done better to have married Annie or almost any woman in the world other than Elspeth Thomson. They were singularly ill-suited. This did not seem so on the surface. They were both dreamers, but were absorbed in their own dreams.

Grahame hoped to enhance his position in the Society he satirized by marrying Elspeth. Had he married his cousin Annie, he would still have been "poor relation". Elspeth thought he had potential, that he could make something of himself or she could make something of him. Apparently his degree of success failed to satisfy her. As for the Society in which he wished to claim his rightful place, Grahame found he much preferred the company of the Riverbank animals.

Both Grahame and Tolkien loved nature. Tolkien had a favorite willow tree as a boy. Sadly, it was cut down. His frequent mention of willows could be an influence from Grahame, a memory of that tree, or an appreciation of the countryside they shared. Love and respect for nature and the past made them conservatives, not so much in an economic, political, or social sense, but in the sense of wanting to conserve and preserve. It follows that they would not be enthusiastic for modern blights such as railways and motorcars. Alastair may have quite liked cars just as Tolkien's sons liked railroads. Cars are used for humor in *The Wind in the Willows*, but they are Toad's temptation and downfall.

Tolkien, like Toad, was a "daring" driver before he gave it up in WWII because of gas rationing. He did not take it up again, having decided roads and cars were destroying the countryside and environment.[6] He said his house in Oxford at Holywell Street, where he lived from 1950 to 1953, was made unlivable by unrelenting streams of motor traffic.[7] He especially enjoyed a holiday in Venice in part because he was "almost free of the cursed disease of the internal combustion engine of which the world is dying".[8] Mr. Bliss, in Tolkien's children's story of that name, had many collisions in his yellow automobile. The *Bodavium Fragments* is also about the destructive effect of cars.[9]

Both writers started by telling stories to amuse their children and ended writing for themselves, to reconcile, understand, and express their deepest beliefs. They found reality in fantasy and reconciled all of the old belief systems. They and their characters enjoyed good food, a pipe, a fireside. Both men lived comfortably but were not materialistic. Their world was male-oriented but was not man or human centered. Grahame found a benevolent force behind nature in the Piper, The Great God Pan. Tolkien found honor and meaning in sacrifice, both in the old myths and in his Catholic faith. Both saw the earth itself as a living thing and all of its inhabitants, including those that had gone before and those yet to come, as deserving of respect. Their world-view is essentially humble. Their main protagonists are small and are unlikely heroes. After daring deeds, they remain humble and small, as, in the scheme of things, all things are. At the end of *The Hobbit* Gandalf told Bilbo: "You are only quite a little fellow in a wide world after all".[10]

This is very like what Eddie Lenihan and Carolyn Eve Green say at the end of *Meeting the Other Crowd*, older stories in the same tradition:

In this age of wonderful technology, when the impossible is almost within our grasp in so many fields of endeavor, how ironic it is that these foregoing stories, from a technologically far more backward era, should still have that one vital lesson to impart to us, without which all our technology will get us nowhere in the end: respect.

For no matter whether the fairies are seen metaphorically or as real beings inhabiting their own real world, a study of them shows us that those who came before us (and many of that mindset still survive) realized that we are—no matter what we may think to the contrary—very little creatures, here for a short time only ("passing through", as the old people say) and that we have no right to destroy what the next generation will most assuredly need to also see itself through.

If only we could learn that lesson, maybe someday we might be worthy of the wisdom of those who knew that to respect the Good People is basically to respect yourself.[11]

When you knock on a door in a hillside or riverbank and are greeted by a hobbit or by a rat or mole with Edwardian clothes and manners, you are meeting the Good People, the Little People, the Other Crowd.

Similarities in the Books

In an early review of the book, Tolkien's friend C.S. Lewis found *The Hobbit* comparable to *The Wind in the Willows*.[1] Lewis was thinking of literary quality and that both books admit the reader into a separate world.

On the surface Grahame's River and the Riverbankers existed in this world and in a specific time and place, Edwardian England. However, his characters also inhabit a separate world, an eternal, timeless never-world that we can always have though it can never be.

Tolkien seems to have grasped the difficulty of classifying *The Wind in the Willows*, though he called it an excellent book and implied an internal integrity. He finally relegated it to the realm of beasty books, I think and hope with reservations. The animals talk as people do, but Grahame had always said that he could understand what small, wild animals were telling him, to Tolkien a magical fairytale element. Grahame's animals were not merely acting the parts of people. Nor were his people wearing the masks of beasts. Both were completely human and completely animal, rather as Christianity explains the duel nature of Christ.

Both Grahame's Riverbank and Tolkien's Middle Earth seem familiar but also far away, 'mysterious and remote', universal but also specific.

One striking and very solid and specific similarity between *The Wind in the Willows* and Tolkien's *Hobbit* and *Lord of the Rings* is the landscape in which the books are set. This is hardly surprising, as the landscape in all three works is in large part derived from that part of the English countryside with which both of these two authors were most familiar. However, the aspects of the landscape that they chose to emphasize, the way in which they depicted it, and the terminology that they used may suggest more than commonality of place.

Prominent, of course, is the River (in Tolkien's books rivers), the willows that grow on its bank, and the reeds that grow at its edge. Grahame originally intended to name his book *The Wind Among the Reeds*. His publisher pointed out that William Butler Yeats had already used this title for a collection of poetry. Grahame was imagining Pan playing his reed pipes. Both he and Tolkien often refer to the sound of the wind in the reeds as well as the trees. Tom Bombadil is Tolkien's Great God Pan. He rescued the hobbits from the Old Forest and gave them shelter in his house, as Pan had sheltered the baby otter on his island in Grahame's chapter "The Piper at the Gates of Dawn". Tom Bombadil always was. "—if all else is conquered, Bombadil will fall, Last as he was First; and then night will come.[2] He sings of reed and willow. There are many reeds and willows along the River Withywindle that ran through the Old Forest. "In the midst of it—willow boughs were creaking."[3] Tom speaks of the willow-man and Old Man Willow's house. He had married the River-daughter.[4]

Later in their journey, the Fellowship of the Ring came to the Great River, Anduin. "On this side of the River they passed forests of great reeds. Dark withered plumes bent and tossed in the light, cold air, hissing softly and sadly."[5]

In *The Two Towers*, Faramir "sat at night by the waters of Anduin in the grey dark under the young, pale moon, watching the ever-moving stream; and the sad reeds were rustling".[6]

Of course, the terrain of the Shire itself had a small river at the base of a hill.

In *The Hobbit*, the adventurers came to a river in the Lone-lands. "Wind got up, and the willows along its banks bent and sighed."[7] Tolkien also wrote in *The Hobbit* of the Land *Beyond*[8], the Wide World[9], and the Wild (Wood?).[10]

Woods in themselves are an important feature of the books, and the authors share a threatening view of them. Tolkien's Old Forest is very like Grahame's Wild Wood. For Mole, alone in the forest, darkness falling made the woods a Shadowland, low and threatening. "Twigs crackled under his feet, logs tripped him, funguses on stumps resembled caricatures",[11] even in the afternoon before he became frightened. At dusk, holes became faces, and the whistling and pattering began. At least for Mole, it was exciting in the beginning, before the woods and the dark started closing in on him. Hobbits never had liked woods, but trees were thinking creatures in Tolkien. They often resented creatures with mobility and wished them ill. "The dark edge of the forest loomed up straight before them. Night seemed to have taken refuge under its great trees, creeping away from the coming dawn."[12] Tolkien wrote of the cold rustle of the wind in the woods[13] and dead leaves on chestnut that rattle mournfully in the night breeze.[14]Tolkien claimed Arthur Rackham's tree drawings as part of his inspiration for Old Man Willow.[15] Rackham was Grahame's first choice to illustrate *The Wind in the Willows*, but Rackham was too busy with other illustrations at the time. He did do illustrations, including drawings of trees, for an edition published in the late 1930's and could be a link between the two writers.

Old Man Willow, ruler of the Old Forest, was a bane to Tom Bambadil, who is seen by Carpenter as the spirit of the vanishing countryside. He was the subject of stories for Tolkien's children and the subject of a poem before becoming part of *The Lord of the Rings*. Old Man Willow once shut Tom up in a crack in its bole with a barrow-wright and a family of badgers.[16] Badger ruled the Wild Wood in the *Wind in the Willows*. In "The Third Adventure of Tom Bombadil", Badger-Brock and his family pull Tom down into their hole.[17] Tom tells the hobbits "an absurd story about badgers and their queer ways".[18]

Grahame's Badger's tunnels were once part of a city built by a previous civilization. In *The Lord of The Rings*, the king dwells under a hill in Mirkwood in halls the dwarfs helped to make long ago.[19] Tolkien calls the dwarfs that built the caves of Moria "busier than badgers".[20] Badgers are shy, seldom-seen creatures but are oddly prominent in the stories of Grahame, Tolkien, and C.S. Lewis. Otter, another major character in *The Wind in the Willows*, is also mentioned by Tolkien. "—choose an otter for swimming".[21]

Badger is not the only Grahame character whose home has counterparts in Tolkien's work. The houses of many of the characters are in the earth, as Anderson also notes.[22] "Hobbits are used to tunneling and being underground".[23] In *The Hobbit*, Bilbo and the dwarfs escape from the elves by way of underground cellars and a trap door in the butler's pantry leading to the river. Rat, Mole, Badger, and Toad retake Toad Hall using a secret passage that leads from the River to a trap door that also happens to be in a butler's pantry.[24]

Grahame's characters would be quite comfortable in hobbit holes. Hobbit homes are in the side of a hill. Rat's house is in the

Riverbank. Mole lived in a hole in the ground like a hobbit. He lived at Mole End. Bilbo Baggins lived at Bag End. Of course, it was not unusual for the English to name a residence—End. It is also true that moles do live in the earth and that river rats live in the banks of rivers. The similarities that relate the books are in the characters and words the authors chose to use. Buggins, a word very close to Baggins, is the brand Rat told the field mice to be sure to buy for the Christmas Eve party at Mole End.[25] Both hobbits and Riverbankers are essentially homebodies who also enjoy an adventure. Both Mole and Bilbo were cleaning house on a nice spring day when their adventures began. Bilbo and Rat are especially torn between love of home and wanderlust. Mole's love of home in "Dolce Domum" can be compared to Frodo's refuge in the "Last Homely House East of the Sea", "—a perfect house, whether you like food or sleep or story-telling or singing or just sitting and thinking best or a pleasant mixture of them all. Merely to be there was a cure for weariness, fear and sadness".[26] Characters in both Grahame and Tolkien often sit by the fire. They love the homey pleasures of good food, a good story, and a pipe to smoke. Bilbo still loved to eat when he was quite senile at Rivendell. Of course, fireside stories could become dull if one did not occasionally have an adventure. Both authors speak of the Wide World, both as a place from which to return "home" and as part of a larger homeland to which adventurers hoped to return after venturing even farther afield, as when the elves visit the Land of Fairie in the West.

Both Grahame and Tolkien use poetry in their books, Tolkien being the better poet. The reader is not treated to the finished poem that Mole encouraged Rat to write to calm himself after Mole had physically restrained him from following the Sea Rat. The poem that Bilbo wrote at Rivendell could be Rat's poem as well.[27] In both

The Wind in the Willows and *The Lord of the Rings*, the sea is almost mythical, a half-forgotten legend, a distant dream. Rivendell had a little of everything, except the sea.[28] The elves will cross the sea to the Gray Havens, which sound very like the Isle of Pan in *The Wind in the Willows*. The Kings of Gondor were descendants of the Kings of Numenor in Westerness, a land that floundered in the sea, perhaps echoing the legend of Atlantis. The wings of Gondor's ancient crown were those of a sea bird, emblem of kings who came over the sea.[29]

Rat had never met anyone who had been to sea. That's why the Sea Rat's stories had such a pull on him. Peter Hunt believes that Mole was off on his own adventure and that Rat stopped him and socialized him to such a degree that Mole in turn restrained Rat when he was bent on going to sea. I have always thought that Mole only wanted to get away from his house-cleaning and into the first of the warm spring sun and air. I had thought that a boat-ride and a picnic and seeing The River was more of an adventure than he had ever hoped to have. Seeing The River was to Mole as going to sea would have been to Rat and as seeing the world was to hobbits.

Gollum might be seen as a darker, more extreme Toad, as what Toad might have become over centuries without such good friends to physically restrain him and pull him back from his misguided ways. Trolls and orcs could be darker stoats and weasels. The arming of Rohan is similar to Grahame's satire on Homeric preparations for war as Rat distributes arms for the storming of Toad Hall.

> The Rat—was running round the room busily, with his arms full of weapons of every kind, distributing them in four little heaps on the floor, and saying excitedly under his breath as he ran: Here's-a-sword-

for-the-Rat, here's-a-sword-for-the-Mole, here's-a-sword-for-the-Toad, here's-a-sword-for-the-Badger! Here's-a-pistol-for-the-Rat, here's-a-pistol-for-the-Mole, here's-a-pistol-for-the-Toad, here's-a-pistol-for-the-Badger! And so on, in a regular, rhythmical way, while the four little heaps gradually grew and grew.[30]

When it began to grow dark, the Rat, with an air of excitement and mystery, summoned them back into the parlour, stood each of them up alongside of his little heap, and proceeded to dress them up for the coming expedition. He was very earnest and thoroughgoing about it, and the affair took quite a long time. First there was a belt to go around each animal, and then a sword to be stuck into each belt, and then a cutlass on the other side to balance it. Then a pair of pistols, a policeman's truncheon, several sets of handcuffs, some bandages and sticking-plaster, a flask and a sandwich-case.[31]

The re-taking of Toad Hall echoes several times in Tolkien's books. The dwarfs return to Lonely Mountain in *The Hobbit*. In *The Return of the King*, the king returns to Gondor, and the hobbits take the Shire back from Saruman. Forgiveness over-rides revenge in all the books. The weasels and stoats are forgiven. Rohan forgave the hillmen who fought for Saruman.[32] As king, Aragorn forgave many orcs and others who were under the power of Mordor. He would have forgiven Saruman. In taking back the Shire, Frodo wanted no killing that could be avoided.[33] He wanted to rescue Lotho, who was occupying Bag End, and did not want Saruman to be killed.

Hobbits are halflings, and so are the animal characters Grahame created. They are literally and figuratively the Little People. They are small and humble and do great deeds. "This quest may be attempted by the weak with as much hope as the strong. Yet such is oft the course of deeds that move the wheels of the world: small hands do them because they must, while the eyes of the great are elsewhere."[34]

The River's Source

There is some aspect of Kenneth Grahame in all of the major *Wind in the Willows* characters, but mostly he is Mole. He tunneled through darkness between the Riverbank and the Bank of England, and there is irony in the fact that the two very different places in which he surfaced were both "banks". Like Grahame, Mole was affable and rather shy. He could fit into various households, social groups, and situations while remaining something of an outsider. Mole End was some little distance from the Riverbank. Mole was not a Riverbanker in the same sense that Rat was. Although he put much of himself into Mole, Grahame's basic model for the character may have been Mr. Pooter, the city clerk from George and Weedon Grossmith's *Diary of a Nobody*, a best-seller of the day.

Rat represents Grahame's romantic, poetic, adventuresome streak. Grahame loved going to Italy. Rat longed to go. The writer also put much of his friends Frederick Furnivall and Edward Atkinson, who were to him as Rat was to Mole, into Mole's friend. Rat, like Mole, may also have a fictional model in a character from Oscar Wilde's book of original fairy tales, *The Happy Prince and Other Stories*. Frederick Furnivall was also Grahame's model when he wished to personify Pan.

There was some of Falstaff and much of Alastair in Toad. The "hearty, flamboyant, gabby, vulgarian" politician Horatio Bottomley added color to the character.[1] Of course, Toad also represents impulses Grahame might have followed had he been less responsible, civilized, and proper. However, Toad must surely be Oscar Wilde in essence. Wilde and Grahame were part of the same literary circle. Like Toad, Wilde was always ready with a toast or a speech at dinners. Like Toad, Wilde was an inveterate non-conformist. Like Toad, Wilde went to jail.

Badger embodies Grahame's tendencies to be a recluse. Grahame saw himself as being, like Badger, awkward in the social situations he could not avoid. Badger was the father Grahame would have liked to have had. He was the father Grahame wanted to be to Alastair. The writer must also have identified with Otter, the father of a son with whom he could not quite cope.

Grahame said that Robert Louis Stevenson was the writer whom he admired most and the one who most influenced him. He may have meant writers among his contemporaries. Both Stevenson and Grahame were contributors to W.E. Henley's *Scots Observer*, which became *The National Observer* when the editorial offices were moved to London in 1890. Henley had Friday dinners at Verrey's Restaurant and Sunday evening gatherings at his house for the *Observer* writers. The two writers must have met at these gatherings before Stevenson's death in 1894. W.B. Yeats was also a contributor and may have been present and may have influenced Grahame in more subtle ways.

Grahame could also have met William Morris, whose work also had a strong influence on him, when both were writing for the *Yellow Book*. Tolkien also claimed Morris, especially his *House of the Wolfings*, as an influence.

Shakespeare, Malory, Sir Thomas Browne, Tennyson, Robert Browning, Matthew Arnold, and Lewis Carroll were also among Grahame's favorite authors.[2] He avidly read the Uncle Remus stories when they came out in 1881. Richard Jeffries, with his whispering reeds, river talk, and talking animals, was also an obvious influence.[3]

Grahame believed that his literary and philosophical roots were primarily in the Classical tradition of Greece and Rome and the stories of Homer. As he also loved modern Italy, he considered the Mediterranean his spiritual home. There had been threads of this tradition in the British islands for a long time. Julius Caesar invaded in 55 and 54 B.C. Although Caesar left an influence, it was the Emperor Claudius who conquered Britain in B.C. 43. An upper class of Romanized Celtic Britons developed. Traders in tin had also exchanged cultural elements even earlier. In the second millennium B.C., pre-Greek and pre-Homeric influences may have reached Britain from the Aegean in the movement of peoples after the island of Thera and Minoan civilization collapsed and after the mainland Mycenean civilization that replaced it conquered Troy. Rumors of Troy's fall could have reached Britain long before Homer.

Grahame's Mediterranean roots were not exclusive. Like Tolkien, he claimed to be greatly influenced by *Beowulf*, although Tolkien was the true scholar of Old Norse Tales. In the 1930's, Tolkien knew *Beowulf* as well as any scholar in the world. He studied the Finnish and Icelandic myths as well. The Norsemen invaded Ireland and brought their stories. *Beowulf* took root in Britain to the south and was written down to be considered the first work of "English" literature.

According to *National Geographic's The Lord of the Ring, Beyond the Movie*, Tolkien wanted to reconstruct an Anglo-Saxon mythical tradition that had existed for England but was lost with the Norman conquest. However, an Anglo-Saxon myth would be Germanic in its roots. Surely some threads of *The Lord of the Rings* must lie in pre-Anglo-Saxon Britain. Major aspects of his inspiration must be akin to one of his first loves, the Welsh language. The Britons were a Celtic people, as are the Welsh, Scots, and Irish. With the Anglo-Saxon conquest of Britain, the Celts and their stories were assimilated, went underground, or were pushed to the Celtic Fringe of Wales, Scotland, and Ireland. Celtic mythology survived best on the separate island of Ireland.

St. Patrick was a Romanized Briton who brought Roman Christianity to Ireland. He sensibly assured its acceptance by combining it with Ireland's fairy religion, a polytheism not so different from the pre-Christian worship of such earth deities as Pan.

Pan was a Romanized, classicized god, but his roots go back to the vague memory of a time before history or civilization, a time even before myth. There are also elements in British and Irish mythology that are echoes in the fog of a pre-Celtic past. Tolkien and Grahame heard these ancient echoes in the mist. Norse, Celtic, and Mediterranean elements had been assimilated into traditions more primitive than myth long before Tolkien decided to create a purely "English" legend.

It is obvious that with migrations and conquests myths intertwined. Very similar stories may also have arisen among widely scattered peoples with no contact. Some mythologists believe that in the beginning and the end there is one basic myth, that of the arisen god/returning king. The king, the greatest of men, was sacrificed to the earth so that the crops would grow. Before the sacrifice was formalized, a better man would kill the king and become king in turn. The old king became a god. Somehow, it was always the same king and the same god, and they became one. As the king gained power, he could have a substitute "king for a day or a year" or perhaps a sacred bull die for him. Abstract gods developed to represent this dying god/returning king. One such god was Pan, with the horns and tail of the sacrificed bull. He represents nature with its death and rebirth. Pan protects all natural things, keeping them safe in the dead months and waking them with his piping in the Spring. In his "VIII Eclogue" Virgil spoke of "Pan, the first who suffered not the reeds to be neglected".[4]

Tolkien, with his emphasis on sacrifice and his returning king, may have considered this the most important if not the first and only myth. Grahame may have basically agreed with this theory of myth as well. His animal characters may be human in effect and civilized, but, as animals, they precede humans, civilization, and myth. They have distinct personalities, but Mole is somehow Everymole. Rat is every rat that has ever been, and Badger is all badgers. Like the arisen god/returning king, they are abstracts of themselves, living forever under the care of Pan.

Beowulf himself is ancient and eternal almost beyond time. His name, bee-wulf, means wolf that steels honey from the bees, a bear.[5] His adventures are paralleled in the Old Norse Saga of *King Hrulf and His Companions*, King Hrulf's chief companion Bothvarr Bjarki is in his deeds Beowulf's counterpart. Bjarki means "little bear". His father is Bjarni, meaning "bear". His mother's name, Bera, means "she-bear". Bothvarr Bjarki is a were-bear. He is a shape-changer and has more than one skin. It is his bear form that goes to battle. It may be that he is of a family of shamans who wear ceremonial bearskins. They might also have gained the designation by looking and fighting like bears.

In *Bear: A Celebration of Power and Beauty*, Rebecca Grambo translates the name of the Danish king Hrulf's companion as Bodvar

Biarki and his father's as Biorn. Biorn's wife turned him into a bear for rejecting her advance. Before being killed by hunters and dogs, Biorn lived in a cave with the girl Bera. Bodvar, third son of Biorn and Bera, appeared to be human but turned into a bear in battle.[6]

The Ainu of Japan and the tribes of Siberia and North America have told stories that relate bears closely to both the human and divine and seem culturally related to each other. Traditions of human/bear shape-shifters and offspring of human/bear unions are geographically wide-spread and make the were-bear a deeply-rooted and nearly universal legend. Many primitive tribes believed themselves to be descended from bears. The medicine society of the Zuni Indians was said to be founded by a half-man/half-bear, and Zuni shamans were thought to have the ability to change into bears. The Southwest Indians also say that Bear Old Man led the first people up from the Lake of Emergence.

The Shasta and Modoc people of the Pacific Northwest believed that when the Great Spirit gave life to the world he made Bear last and gave him dominion over creation. Bear was so strong and fierce he chased the Great Spirit back to the heavens.[7] The Great Spirit later decided to live on the earth for a while and turned Mt. Shasta into a tipi. One night he sent his youngest daughter to the top of the tipi to tell a violent storm to blow more gently. In trying to see the ocean, she fell into the forest below. The forest, of course, was owned and ruled by bears. At that time bears talked and walked upright and wielded clubs. A bear found the child and took her home to his wife, who was a wise woman among the bears and would know what to do. She said she would raise her as her own. When the girl grew up, she married the couple's son. Her children were the first Indians.[8]

The bears all loved these part-bear/part-divine children and built them a beautiful lodge. When the bear mother thought she would soon die, she asked the Great Spirit to come down from Mt. Shasta so that she could tell him what had become of his daughter and rest in peace. He was furious that the bears had created a new race, his prerogative. The story is not unlike *Genesis* in that he made the children leave their lodge and sent them into the world. He took his daughter back to Mt. Shasta. He told the bears to be quiet, to drop their clubs, and to walk on all fours till he returned to free them. He never came back.

Of course, Bear's true home is in the heavens with the Great Bear constellation, Ursa Major. The people of Northwest Siberia say that the first bear was child of the heavenly father. She came down to earth and taught men the ceremony that sends the earthly bears they kill home to the heavens.[9]

There is also an aspect of the myth of the eternal return in bear legends. The Great Bear of the sky goes through the cycle of the hunt and returns. The earthly bear goes into the earth and is as dead in winter and is resurrected in the spring. He was often considered to be a willing sacrifice, sometimes raised in royal style for that purpose and sometimes treated as king for the day. He left his body to sustain man's life and his spirit as man's protector. In killing a bear, man freed him to go home to the sky from where he would return to begin the cycle of their relationship again.

Rebecca Grambo relates a story that John Staal told about bears and also trees that are very like Tolkien's walking, talking ents. In a forest of great oaks, the trees walk around and visit each other between sunset and sunrise. A bear, also a night wanderer but a stranger in the wild wood, bumped into a moving tree and did not known to apologize. The tree chased him, reminding us of the terrors of the forest at night and further confusing and frightening the bear.

It caught him just before sunrise and threw him into the sky to be the Great Bear constellation.[10]

Great Bear of the Sky, King of the Forest, and immortal and willing sacrifice to save and sustain man, it is little wonder that Bear is a fit name for heroes (Beowulf) and kings (Artois/Arthur) and was an inspiration to Tolkien and Grahame.

Beorn, in Tolkien's *The Hobbit*, is a were-bear, modeled on Bothvarr Bjarki and, through him, on Beowulf. Beorn is "immensely strong, a honey-eater, man by day but bear by night, capable of appearing in battle in bear's shape".[11] As would be expected in a man-bear, Beorn is gruff but good-humored and ferocious but kind-hearted. He is insufficiently socialized but easily amused. He is a vegetarian and an environmentalist. Yet there is something very primitive about Beorn. Beneath his kind good humor lurks a dark danger that we don't quite understand. Beorn is from the merciless world before fairy tale.[12]

The name Beorn is the Old English equivalent of Bjarni. In Old English, it means man, but it once meant bear. Ironically, Beowulf means bear, not wolf. Grahame = grey coat = wolf. Of course, all of Grahame's animal characters in *Wind in the Willows* are half-human were-animals. Beorn is not Tolkien's only example. He calls his dragon Smaug a were-worm in *The Hobbit*.

Tolkien's trolls were made in darkness in imitation of the tree-tending ents. Orcs were likewise made in imitation of elves.[13] Elves were Tolkien's ideal beings. They may have a source in Ireland's Tuatha de Danann, possibly a pre-Celtic race which survived in lore as tall, shining fairies. His dwarfs are much like Irish Gnomes.[14] The Celts may have driven pre-Celtic tribes literally underground, and Druids may have dwelt in chambered mounds very like hobbit houses.[15] In *Meeting the Other Crowd* a girl carried off by fairies is brought to a door in a hill (very much like a hobbit house) for a

November Eve (Halloween) dance (or sacrifice?).[16] Tolkien himself calls hobbits "the little people".[17] However, he also mentions fairies as something apart from solid, sensible, down-to-earth hobbits. The Took family of hobbits, to which Bilbo's mother belonged, was known to be a little fey. Tolkien says their ancestor must have taken a fairy wife.[18] They occasionally went on adventures. (Off with the fairies?)

Tolkien had ties with Ireland. After World War II, he restricted his work as an external examiner to Ireland's Catholic University. He toured the country and made many friends there.[19] He shared many interests with the Irish and would have been comfortable among them. They shared the Catholic religion but a love of pagan traditions as well. Tolkien loved Celtic languages as well as Celtic myth. He would have loved the male conviviality of Irish pub life and the Irish love of stories, poetry, and song. Catholic University awarded him an honorary doctorate of letters in 1954.[20] Rather than trying to reconstruct his missing English myth by working backwards, Tolkien might have done as well to look for it in Ireland.

Consciously or not, perhaps he did. Britons took their stories with them when they were driven by invasions to the Celtic Fringe. Englishmen of Grahame's and Tolkien's generations may in part have brought the stories back.

Grahame and his cousin Annie shared a love of the old Scottish stories and songs. However, Celtic stories were rediscovered or reconstructed mostly in Ireland. Oscar Wilde's mother, Lady Jane Francesca Elgee Wilde, was a writer and an avid collector of Irish stories. Her son Oscar's book *The Happy Prince*, in which Grahame found an inspiration for Rat, is a collection of original fairytales. However, Wilde must have been influenced by his mother's work. William Butler Yeats, known primarily as a poet, was born in England

and raised in Ireland. He returned to Ireland and devoted himself to its culture and stories. He gentrified the fairies as Grahame gentrified moles and rats. Grahame would have had a social acquaintance with both Wilde and Yeats through his literary connections and was familiar with their work.

It is probable that Tolkien was also familiar with Yeat's work. In Tolkien, trees of silver and gold bloomed in the world's youth.[21] This suggests Yeat's "golden apples of the sun, silver apples of the moon" as well as images of Eden. Tolkien toyed with the idea of making the sun and moon be from the last fruits of the two trees of Valinor.[22] Although there were other images and possible sources aside from Yeats, that the hobbits returned home to find that the harvest had gone out of the Shire under Saruman as it had gone out of Ireland during the famine suggests that Tolkien had a knowledge of and sympathy for Irish history.[23]

Perhaps there is only one story. Perhaps the return of the king is the basic myth after all. Aragon was obviously the king returned. Is it then a part of Grahame's irony that his returning king was a toad and not a well-behaved toad at that? Is it a political statement from "conservative" Grahame that the king must be watched, even confined, by his friends? Although hobbits are unusual heroes, they are not so unlikely as a mole and a rat. Will the last be first when the kingdom is established on earth, or will heroes return to their firesides and lead quiet lives again? Does power always corrupt when retained, even in the Garden?

Toads don't drive motor cars. Middle Earth probably never existed except in the imaginations of Tolkien and all of us who accompanied him on his quest. Eden probably never existed either, at least not as we imagine it. But a river runs from it, through Middle Earth and all the world.

The Wild Wood

A river is often a central feature in old legends because commerce, travel, and settlement were by way of rivers. The forest was a sinister and threatening presence surrounding these settlements. This path of settlement is clearly shown in *The House of the Wolfings* by William Morris, who was interested in pre-industrial craftsmanship and society and in social utopia and was claimed as an influence by both Grahame and Tolkien. Grahame and Morris were contemporaries for the first part of Grahame's life, Morris dying in 1887. Grahame may have been more interested in Morris's utopian writing, and the fact that Grahame used Otter as a major character and Otter was the name of a war leader in *The House of the Wolfings* might have been coincidence, as might the fact that the forest around Morris's settlement was called the wild-wood.

Although *The House of the Wolfings* is a heroic story of the joy of war and the glory of death in battle, there is hope expressed near the end of future utopian peace. Arinborn, chief of the Bearings, a clan whose homestead has already been destroyed, says "—it is to me as if the kindreds that I love had filled the whole earth and left no room for foeman: even so it may really be some day".[1] Such a sentiment would have found an empathic reader in both Grahame and Tolkien.

Morris's book is a romance in prose and verse, and both Grahame and Tolkien use verse in their writing.

Tolkien named this specific book among Morris's works as especially impressing and influencing him. The Wolfings and Bearings are among the tribes or extended families of Goths that came down Mirkwood-water, a river that ran through Mirkwood, the proper name of the surrounding wild-wood. Mirkwood is a name from ancient Germanic geography and legend[2] and is, of course, also used by Tolkien.

In *The Hobbit*, Mirkwood is the greatest forest of the northern world. It was over the Edge of the Wild.[3] The way through was dark, dangerous, and difficult. Wild things there were strange and savage. Beorn doubted they would find anything wholesome to eat or drink.[4] It was still and seemed airless. A narrow path wound through shadows and among trees with huge, gnarled trunks and twisted branches. Strange noises and eyes that gleamed and disappeared in the pitch dark of night are reminiscent of Mole's venture into the Wild Wood in *The Wind in the Willows*. In Needle's 1981 book that presents the other side of the *Wind in the Willows* story Baxter Ferret describes the Wild Wood much as Tolkien describes Mirkwood.

> The Wild Wood, when I finally entered it, seemed to have grown darker, bleaker, blacker than I could ever remember it. There were no animals about, no birds. Nothing edible grew, nothing but the tall hard trees that soughed in the bitter wind, occasionally dropping great clouts of snow that crashed from high branches into what meager undergrowth rose out of the drifts.[5]

Among the clans that came down Morris's Mirkwood-water were the Bearings, the Elkings, and, perhaps significant in terms of influence on Grahame, the Willow-bush and the Water-bank. They cleared and settled three marks, a mark being land held in common among medieval Germanic tribes. A clan's main dwelling was called the house or roof. It was surrounded by cots for slaves or thralls taken in battle and for young men who wanted to be more independent of the group. The Wolfings were among those who had their House in the Mid-mark. This may relate it to Middle Earth, as does the fact that, although the attackers are called Romans, the time and place in which the story is set are illusive. The prophetess Hall-sun speaks to her father of the last of his days on Mid-earth.[6]

The names of the clans are the signs under which they fight. There is no suggestion that they go into battle dressed as wolves, bear, or elk or that they change their shape. However, Hall-sun and her mother Wood-sun have the blood of the gods and are shape-changers as well as seers. They are very like Tolkien's elves.

Tolkien must have been thinking about *The House of the Wolfings*, particularly when he wrote about the Riders of Rohan, who were also "Men of the Mark". Thiodolf was leader of the Wolfings and chief of the Mark. In Tolkien's *The Return of the King*, Theoden is King of the Mark. Both die, as kings of the eternal return, fighting for their people. Thiodolf believes that it is his fate to die for the Wolfings. "What life for the life of the people shall be given once for all?"[7] Wood-sun, in love with him, tells him he will be of more use to them if he lives to fight again and gives him a magic hauberk or coat of mail made by dwarfs in ancient times. Might this be a prototype for a magic vest made by elves and worn by Bilbo and Frodo? The hauberk is cursed as well as blessed, and Thiodolf grows faint when he wears it. He discards it and dies, but, as with Arthur and all true kings, it is said he is only sleeping in his burial mound and will return when the Goths need him most.

Wood-sun said she had not been truly of the gods since the day she and Thiodolf became lovers in the sacred grove and she conceived their daughter Hall-sun. This is echoed in the elfin daughter Arwen, who is willing to become a mortal for Aragorn in *The Lord of the Rings*.

Like King Theoden's daughter Eowyn, the Hall-sun was left in charge when the army went off to fight. Eowyn longed to join the warriors. The Hall-sun successfully led the stay-at-homes in a battle to defend the House.

As a seer, the Hall-sun had an unclear vision in which images of what had been and what then was suggested things to be.[8] This is similar to Tolkien's "things that are and things that were and some things yet to be" seen in the mirror of Galadriel. Grahame must have found affinity in Hall-sun's "I knew the beasts' desires as though in words they spoke".[9]

Rings have timeless and universal magic, as they have no beginning or end. Beowulf came to help the Ring-Danes. Their king was the ring giver. Their wealth was the ring hoard. When Thiodolf was made war-leader of the Folk in *The House of the Wolfings*, he wore a ring (armband) made by the dwarfs that signified his leadership. His co-leader, Otter, sent his ring as a token when he sent Geirbald to find Thiodolf. Otter had sent Gisli (a name similar to Gimli) o f the Upper Mark with news of a victory over the Romans in an oak grove, an ancient, holy place, early in the war. The grove where Thiodolf and Wood-sun met and became lovers was of hazel, another magic wood. These rings of trees around clearings were the most ancient places of magic, worship, and sacrifice. In Mary Stewart's book *The Crystal Cave*, young Merlin came upon a sacrifice in such a grove. Not only these groves in the forest but individual trees and even leaves were considered by most early people to have their own intelligence, souls, and magical powers. In Morris's book, the clan's house or roof as a physical structure is thought to have its own life, intelligence, and memory, derived in part perhaps from the ongoing life of the clan and in part from the life of the trees from which it was made. "The house remembered old stories told within it that men had forgot."[10]

The name Bambi is familiar to everyone. The name Felix Salten is not. Bambi was so completely taken over by Disney that many people are unaware that the original books, *Bambi* and *Bambi's Children*, written by Felix Salten in the 1920's and 1930's, are books that can be appreciated by older children and adults who may have become too sophisticated for the Disney characters.

I don't know if Felix Salten was familiar with *The Wind in the Willows* or Grahame's talking animals. Chapter 20 of *Bambi* is suggestive of *The Wind in the Willows*." Bambi was alone. He walked beside the water that ran swiftly among the reeds and swamp-willows."[11] Watching a family of ducks is reminiscent of Oscar Wilde's story *The Devoted Friend*, from which Grahame in part derived Ratty. Willows and ducks also appear in *Bambi's Children*.

The Devoted Friend is not about friendship at all but about one person using another. Grahame made it into a story of true friendship, although Ratty does without effort make Mole feel privileged to load the picnic hamper on the boat and repack it after the picnic. This was early in the book, perhaps before Grahame had decided where to go with the inspiration Wilde had given him.

In some ways Salten is closer to the sadness of Wilde's stories and the nobility of his talking birds. If *The Wind in the Willows* is about friendship, *Bambi* is about being alone, ironically something that Grahame understood quite well. Grahame admired animals for being true to their nature and therefore would have approved of Salten's presentation of them. However, Grahame and Salten were not really writing in the same tradition. Salten's animals use human speech and refer to each other as people, but they are not halflings. There are no fairies in *Bambi*. Salten did not create a mythology or write in the mythic tradition. He wrote of the cycle of life and the seasons and of animals as they actually live in the forest. He wrote of beauty and joy but also with stark reality of pain, hunger, death, and ultimate aloneness. The animals view man as a mythic, supernatural, all-powerful being, but the Old Stag shows Bambi that men can bleed and die as the forest creatures do.

Bambi's forest is not a very wild Wild Wood. Elk are the only animals larger than the deer, and they seem to occasionally pass through rather than being permanent residents. The major predator is the fox. A neglected dog takes to the woods and the wolf-like ways of its ancestors. A feral cat stalks the forest to kill for fun and is therefore considered a demon. None of the naturally wild animals are evil, but one who lives peaceably with his neighbors in the season of plenty will eat them in the season of want. If there is a myth involved, it is the basic myth of the eternal return. Like Grahame's animals, Salten's have a universal aspect. Squirrel is still Squirrel through generations, although one gains the name Perri in *Bambi's Children*. Fox is hunted down, but there is still Fox. Bambi becomes the Old Stag. The cycle of life continues in the stark face of death.

Squirrel's beautiful old oak tree is treated as a feeling, conscious being in *Bambi*. Man cut it down, leaving Squirrel and its other residents homeless. "The tree groaned aloud when it was wounded. It kept on groaning, and the tooth kept gnawing. It was dreadful to hear."[12] In *Bambi*, this can be viewed as the perception of the animals, but that trees have personality, souls, feelings, voices, and magic power is nearly universal in ancient belief. Bambi's son Geno thought he heard the trees speak, but he was half asleep.[13]

In Tolkien's *The Two Towers*, Treebeard laments of the trees cut down by Saruman, "Many had voices of their own that are lost forever now".[14] Tolkien's trees have souls or spirits as well as voices. Primitive people believed trees had souls and an afterlife. Ancient Greek philosophers attributed intellect and sense to trees. It seemed natural that trees, having been given souls, should have the power of speech, from silent speech to creaking in the branches and rustling of the wind in the leaves to human speech.[15] Of course, the perceived speech of trees could also have suggested they have souls.

Individual leaves have also been thought to have souls or be inhabited by living beings. Probably because of their rustling, whispering sound they were thought to know all secrets.[16] The first temples were groves, circles of trees around clearings, usually in high places. They were occupied by supernatural beings, whose voices were heard in the creaking of the branches and the rustling of the leaves in the wind.[17] The whitethorn tree is the entrance to the other world in Celtic myth. A fairy path is a straight path between whitethorns, usually in a fairy fort, the Irish term for the ancient sacred grove. As will be seen in "The Dark Side of Fairie", fairy forts could make an impact on this world as late as 1895.

Trees are now generally seen as peaceful and benevolent, but in myths around the world, spirits that dwell in them often mean harm. Fear of the forest was widespread, less for wild animals and hidden enemies than for spirit dwellers. Spirits of the dead were sometimes thought to inhabit trees. The fire god dwelled there as well. Ancient myths say the hawthorn originated from lightning. Fire may have started when two branches rubbed together in a storm.[18] Man eventually realized that he could rub twigs together and have fire when he wanted it and thus gained some control of the power that lived in trees.

The word forest may come from the Latin foris, meaning only the out-of-doors or unenclosed land, or from the Welsh gores or gorest, meaning waste or unsettled land, often over-grown with trees.[19] Both imply outside home and hearth and beyond protection. The first settlers in America had a concept of the forest as something to be fought back and overcome, something to be settled, something other. Besides being beyond the circle of protection, there has always been a perception that the forest draws in on itself and stands guard to protect its inhabitants against intruders. We see in *Bambi* that this is not a myth but largely true.

The Geni or Spirit of the Forest lived in a tree, usually an old and gnarled one, and protected the trees and forest. This tree was King of the Forest. For Tolkien, this is the ent Treebeard or Fangorn. "Cut no living wood in the ancient forest of Fangorn", warned Aragorn. A tree seemed to warm itself by the fire made of dead wood.[20] Ents appear as being half tree and half troll and are the oldest living beings and the shepherds of the trees. Some trees are indeed ancient. California's Sequoia, a cypress, is from the Mesozoic Epoch and the oldest thing still living on the earth.[21] Treebeard saw the earth as a living thing. He spoke of the roots of the mountain and the mountain's feet and arms. Ents are the earthborn and as old as the mountains. It is Treebeard and Gandalf who speak for Tolkien as a conservationist. "All worthy things that are in peril as the world now stands, those are my care", says Gandalf.[22] "There are other men and other lives and time still to be."[23] The Third Age of the World was ending. The Fourth Age would be of men. "Preserve what may be preserved. Though much has been saved, much must now pass away."[24] This echoes King Theoden's fear that "much that was fair and wonderful shall pass forever out of Middle Earth".[25] Like Morris and Grahame, Tolkien deplored industrialization. When they return home, the hobbits regret that trees have been cut down by Saruman for ugly new houses for workers in his industry.

Many cultures have a tradition that man is descended from a tree.[26] Bambi equated a stag's rack with the branches of a tree and said deer and trees are close relatives, especially as a stag loses his antlers as a tree loses its leaves and both return next year. Antlers and branches become stronger and more numerous through death and rebirth. When Gandalf told Theoden about the ents, the king said, "Out of the shadows of legend I begin a little to understand the marvel of the trees".[27]

Treebeard loved the rowen tree. The rowen or quicken tree grew in the Land of Forever Young of Irish legend. The Tuatha de Danaan, who would become the Good People, were bringing berries from the tree from the Land of Fairie and dropped one in the Wood of Dooros in County Sligo. The berry grew into a great tree with the magical properties of those the fairies grew. Its berries were sweet as honey and had the effect of wine. If a very old person ate three, he would again be 30 (or perhaps only feel as if he were). The giant Shavan guarded the tree, and, as everyone was afraid of him, a wilderness grew up for miles around.[28] This legend gave substance to the sense of forbidden or alien territory that a forest can evoke and that is sensed in the books of Grahame and Tolkien. As the hobbits listened to Tom Bombadil, "they began to understand the lives of the Forest apart from themselves, indeed to feel themselves the strangers where all other things were at home".[29] This was the realm of Old Man Willow, who, evocative of *The Wind in the Willows*, was "a master of the winds, and his song and thought ran through the woods on both sides of the river".[30]

Legends of the willow long pre-dated Tolkien or Grahame. Of course, as Grahame's original choice of a title was *The Wind Among the Reeds*, he may have been referring to river willows that grow in the river near the bank as reeds do and not the tree at all. The enchantress Circe lived in a willow grove. A weeping willow sprang from the tears King David shed for forty days in remorse for his sin. It was often used in place of a hazel branch as a divining rod or magic wand. The willow and the mistletoe that grows on it are sacred to the Ainu of Japan. The oak and the ash trees are also often considered sacred and magical and are represented in myth and legend. *Beowulf* may not be the only story from Scandinavia to take root in the British Isles. In Norway, Axel Thordsen and the Fair Valdberg never united in life, but ash trees planted on their graves entwined,[31] as did the rose and brier in the old and still well-known ballad "Barbara Allen".

In John Gardner's *Grendel*, an old priest walks with a cane of ash. "He thinks it has magic in it."[32] Grendel emerges like a dark shadow from the forest, called the dismal wood in Beowulf. Like an unseen shadow, he watched the Danes from the forest eaves. Grendel *is* Beowulf from the monster's point of view. A descendant of Cain, he represents the other, the non-Christian, paganism, nature, the earth, and the forest at its most sinister. He is not a passive protector of the forest, but its avenger. Men destroy the forest and each other, giving Grendel self-justification for attacking them. The monster is moved but sickened by the heroic songs in which men glorify their bloody deeds. "No wolf was so vicious to other wolves."[33] The book is a satire on *Beowulf* and by extension on *The House of the Wolfings* and all the old heroic tales. "Did they murder each other more gently because in the woods sweet songbirds sang?"[34]

The forest and trees have magical aspects in *Grendel*. Seeing the monster stuck between the boles of two trees, men thought he was an oak tree spirit. The twisted limbs of trees seal in drab secrets.[35] "The forest whispered back—yet not the forest, something deeper, an impression from another mind, some live thing old and terrible."[36]

Published in 1971, *Grendel* could have been influenced by Grahame and Tolkien, but, of course, was mostly influenced by *Beowulf*. Like hobbits and Grahame's animals, Grendel lives underground. The woods are above and the cavern river far below. His tunnels are not unlike Badger's but are more like Gollum's lair, as there is a lake or pool. Grendel can be seen as Gollum grown large and Gollum as a shrunken Grendel. Grendel is related to men as Gollum is related to hobbits.

Like the noble Bambi, Grendel was alone. So in the end was his rival Hrothgar. So ultimately was Beowulf.

In Stephen King's *The Girl Who Loved Tom Gordon*, a nine-year-old lost in the northern New England woods is very much alone and expresses well the foreboding feel of the forest that was so well captured by Grahame and also by Wyke-Smith in *The Marvelous Land of Snergs* with its twisted trees and, of course, by Tolkien. King mentions *The Wind in the Willows*[37], *The Hobbit*[38], Bilbo Baggins and the Misty Mountains.[39] As King's heroine, Trish, became exhausted, she saw intelligence and malevolent intent in obstructing bushes.[40] Trees blurred into threatening shapes as darkness fell[41] and moonlight gave them bone faces.[42] "Sometimes when people got lost in the woods, they got seriously hurt. Sometimes they died."[43] Trish had come upon a beaver colony in her trek through the woods, and her delight made her forget her situation and fear for the moment. The head beaver reminded her of illustrations she had seen in *The Wind in the Willows*.[44] Stephen King doesn't tell us if Trish remembered how frightened Mole was when he was lost in the woods at night, but the reference to the illustrations tells us that King consciously remembered Grahame's book. Toad, too, found the forest to be a frightening place when he spent the night there after escaping from prison.

The forest is also important in T.H. White's interpretation of the Arthurian legend, *The Once and Future King*. Arthur was raised in Sir Hector's castle in the Forest Savage. Like Mole, the future king got lost in the woods and spent the night there. Next morning he met the wizard Merlin who became his tutor and changed him into animals to help him understand the world. Later Arthur and Sir Hector's son Kay went into the woods seeking an adventure and met Robin 'ood (Wood, not Hood), another Pan-like protector of the forest.

In Mary Stewart's trilogy on the Arthurian legend, Merlin brought a stone from the sacred circle of Killare, the heart of Ireland, to Stonehenge to be the grave stone of King Ambrosius. Where trees did not form sacred groves, standing stones were erected in sacred circles that were called Dances.

Behind the ents and Old Man Willow and even the monster Grendel and the much more benign Robin 'ood is the myth of the great god Pan. Being born of the god Hermes, god of travel, and a wood-nymph, he is a traveler but is at home in the forest. Like the voices of the trees, his pipes are only clearly heard in a dream state, often at "The Gates of Dawn". Like the woods itself, he remains mysterious, alien, wild, and elusive. He is always just ahead of us, just beyond clear sight, like a shadow that slips among the trees or sunlight through the branches shining on the forest floor. Although he seems etereal he is deeply and firmly rooted in the past and remains a real and solid presence in the world.

The Dark Side of Fairie

In 1894, a play by William Butler Yeats was produced. It was called *The Land of Heart's Desire* and was set in County Sligo on a windy May Eve a century before. It would not have been credible to have it happen in the modern, sophisticated 1890's. In the play, a young bride is reading an old book or manuscript that she has found. In the story she is reading, an Irish princess hears a voice singing on such a May Eve and follows it to the land of Fairie, Tir na n'Og, where no one gets old. She is there still, dancing "deep in the dewy shadow of a wood or where stars walk upon a mountain-top".[1] In *The Wind in the Willows*, the song of the reeds is dance music, played on Pan's pipes.[2]

The bride in Yeats' play and her young husband are living with his parents in a small farmhouse. The young couple seem to be in love, but the bride regrets her loss of freedom and is not content with the prospect of growing old in a limited life of drudgery such as her mother-in-law has had. A child is heard at the door and is let in out of the cold wind. She is a fairy child, and she has come for the discontented bride, who is torn between going and staying. She dies, and her spirit leaves with the child.

Yeats' play bombed badly. The 1890's were too modern and sophisticated for such nonsense. A year later, in the south riding of County Tipperary, South Tip as it was called, Bridget Cleary died.

To outward appearances, the Clearys were especially modern and sophisticated for their time and place. Bridget, like the bride of Yeats' play, was a young woman of independent spirit. Attractive and intelligent, she had done well in her eight or nine years of convent school. She was then apprenticed to a dressmaker, probably in the region's fairly large town of Clonmel. Her parents, Patrick and Bridget Boland, were modern and forward-looking enough to want her to be able to earn a living. She did not, however, immediately become a dressmaker. She worked for a time as a housekeeper in the village of Cloneen.

Michael Cleary, a cooper by trade, also went to Clonmel but, times being bad, did not find steady work there either. He settled near Cloneen and became something of an itinerant cooper, taking jobs in Clonmel when he could get them and odd jobs other places when he could not. In Clonmel or Cloneen, he met Bridget. They were married in 1887 and a year later moved in with the Bolands, Bridget's parents, who had qualified for a government-built laborer's cottage, very like the cottage in Yeats' play but with three rooms rather than two. It would have been considered quite adequate for two couples, and the younger couple could save money for a more independent life in the future. Michael continued to travel in his work during the week and also had a shop on the property. Bridget raised chickens and sold eggs and did sewing at home, the family having made the considerable investment of buying a Singer machine. She also covered a fairly large territory in daily walks to deliver eggs and finished sewing. On these walks, she often took a detour to visit her favorite fairy fort, which was located on Scanlon's Field.

Fairy forts were groves of trees growing in a ring around an ancient moat with a clearing in the center. Bridget favored the smaller of two such groves on Kylnagranagh Hill. She visited it often after her mother died in February 1894. She also showed more interest in fairy lore. Perhaps she felt an obligation to take up her mother's mantle in this respect, her mother being well versed in the ways of the Good People. Her mother's death left the younger Bridget the woman of a house often full of men. No record has been found of where her three older brothers, who had apparently left the area, had gone or when they died.[3] However, the house was a gathering place for male relatives. Bridget may have wanted a quiet place to be alone and remember her mother, whose companionship she undoubtedly missed. Bridget had always been active and energetic, but her mother's death would have added an additional burden of housework to her other enterprises, especially as she was also preparing a place to raise pigs.

On Wednesday, March 6, 1895, Bridget set out to deliver eggs. She said she waited two hours to collect money from her relative John Dunne, who was not at home. He was an expert in the fairy traditions and lived near her favorite fairy fort. It is likely that she went there. The unpredictable March weather had turned colder. She could easily have taken a chill. She sat shivering by the fire, which could not warm her, when she finally returned home. She seemed distracted and said she ached and felt ill. The next day, she was in bed with fever, headache, and congestion. Saturday, March 9, she went out briefly to supervise a man who had been hired to plow the garden. This brought on another bout of severe chills, and her condition worsened. She may well have had pneumonia. Tuberculosis has been suggested but is unlikely. By all accounts, she had never been ill. If she had never known illness and had been immersing herself in fairy lore, being suddenly struck by serious sickness may have made her half suspect that she had been struck by the Si Gaoith or fairy wind, akin perhaps to the whirlwind of Job.

At times during her illness she seemed to taunt Michael in his contention that she was not his wife but a changling and the true Bridget had been taken by the fairies to the fairy world. She knew she was not herself. She knew she had changed. Might part of her fevered brain have thought she might be a changling?

Michael went to great trouble in trying to get the doctor to come. When he finally came, he thought Bridget was nervous and agitated and might have slight bronchitis but was not seriously ill. He did her no good. The priest proved of no use either. The frustrated husband went "out the mountain" to obtain cures and incantations from a fairy doctor. Slievenamon, the mountain that dominates the area where the Clearys lived, had long been steeped in Fairie beliefs. Days were now spent in forcing bitter herbs down a woman who was probably too sick to swallow, throwing urine on her, threatening her with fire, trying to make her prove that she was still human by forcing her to eat human food, and asking repeatedly in various ways, "Are you a witch, or are you a fairy, or are you the wife of Michael Cleary?"

The night of March 15, Bridget got dressed and sat at the hearth drinking tea with Michael, her father, her aunt Mary, her cousin Johanna, and Johanna's daughter Katie. Her cousins, Michael, Patrick, and William, were sleeping in one of the two small bedrooms. This was the ninth day since Bridget had "gone with the fairies". Three times three was a magical and fatal number. The ninth day was the last chance to bring her back without resorting to even more drastic measures. The cottage had been filled with relatives and neighbors most of the time since Bridget had taken ill. Her illness and attempted cure was the only show in the countryside. All had agreed with

Michael that she was not herself and must be a changling. Those there that night seemed to think that the cures and rituals had finally worked and it really was their Bridget. Michael was less sure. He insisted that she give a final proof by eating three pieces of bread and jam, three being a magical number. She ate the first two and twice answered that she was not a witch or fairy but Michael's wife. Either she was too ill to eat the third piece or too angry and disgusted at her husband's foolishness to continue. He threw her to the floor, and she hit her head on a flagstone in front of the hearth. He then knelt on her chest and tried to force the bread down her throat. He held a burning stick from the fire over her mouth. She was still conscious, as she managed to turn to the side and whisper to her cousin, "Oh, Han, Han". Those words were the last sound she made.

"Begor, Han! I believe she's dead", said Michael, according to Johanna's trial testimony. It is comforting to believe he was right. She made no sound or protest or sign of pain when he poured paraffin oil from a lamp on her and set her on fire. She was weakened from well over a week of illness and torture. If she was not dead already, the shock of the fire probably would have killed her instantly even had she not hit her head and been choked. It took the paraffin half an hour to burn off. Michael had still not given up trying to get his wife back. He had her father, who said he would do anything to bring back his child, and her cousin Patrick help him lift her onto the grate, the theory being that the changling would go up the chimney and their Bridget would return to them healthy and whole. The mid part of her body burned for another half hour on the grate, burned nearly through in places. "Nothing but smoke went up the chimney."[4] Fairy, witch, or wife, in the early morning hours of March 16, the body on the grate was dead. Michael and her cousin Patrick buried her in a shallow grave.

Michael still insisted that the real Bridget was being held at the fairy fort. He led a group of rescuers there the next night, the eve of St. Patrick's Day, to pull Bridget off her horse when she rode out with the fairies. No fairies appeared. Michael returned, however, the next night and the next. He was arrested on March 20.

In *The Wind in the Willows*, Otter waited night after night at the ford in the river where his son Portly loved to go after Portly disappeared. This is reminiscent of Michael Cleary waiting at Bridget's favorite fairy fort after he had apparently killed her. Bridget was with the fairies. Portly was with the Great God Pan. But Portly was returned unharmed in the better world of the Riverbank.

So Otter goes there every night and watches—on the chance you know, just the chance.[5]

Michael Cleary's persistence argues for his belief in the fairy traditions, as does the fact that his mother was said to have "gone with the fairies" for a time when she was young. What Michael did to Bridget seems cruel treatment even if she were a changling. The jury apparently believed Michael's stated motives. He was found guilty of manslaughter and sentenced to twenty years, of which he served fifteen. We cannot know Bridget's thoughts or her interpretation of her sudden illness. We do know it was a strong tradition that led her husband to act as he did and to do so with impunity in the presence of family and neighbors.

The tradition of being taken by the fairies is not entirely confined to Irish stories.

In the 14th century verse romance "Sir Orfus", a variation of the Greek myth "Orpheus and Eurydice," Lady Heurodis was stolen by fairies.[6]

Lenihan relates in *Meeting the Other Crowd* that, about a quarter of a century before the Cleary case, a woman was knocked down by the Si Gaoith and was never herself again. Her husband sought the advice of Biddy Early, a practitioner in the Fairie arts. She told him his wife would be dead when he got home and gave him a stick with which to beat the corpse. He threw out the mourners and did so. The fairy woman went out the back door, and his wife came in the front, alive and young.[7]

In the story *A Girl carried by the Fairies*, a dead girl could be pulled off a white Fairy horse and brought back.[8] In Celtic tradition, meeting a white animal was often followed by an encounter with Fairie.

Lady Wilde collected the story *The Stolen Bride*, in which the Kern of Querin rescued a girl who was about to be married when the Fairies cast a death-like spell upon her and carried her off on a brier on November Eve. Like May Eve, November Eve is a time of special power for the Good Folk. As in Yeat's play, it seems one had best be dead or in a death-like trance to "go with the Fairies". If we know anything about Bridget Cleary, we know that she wanted things other than what she had. By killing her, her husband was more likely to send her to "The Land of Heart's Desire" than to bring her back. The fairy and ghost worlds often come together on the other side.[9]

The Cleary trial was front-page news around the world. Americans were prejudiced against the Irish and other Catholics and did not fully integrate them into the country's mainstream society. Thus they knew little about mainstream America's ways. The larger America knew even less about the segregated Irish and less yet about the Fairie tradition. After the Cleary scandal, Americans were even more prejudiced and confused. Well into the 20th century, long after the details of the case and the name Cleary were forgot, faint rumors lingered like whispers in the wind or vague echoes of the Si Gaoith that hit South Tip in 1895. "Catholics still burn witches in Ireland."

The Cleary case killed the pending Home Rule Bill for Ireland. Such "simple" people could not be left to rule themselves. It mattered little if Bridget Cleary was struck by the Si Gaoith or a more earthly March wind. It was a wind of great destruction. It had the primitive force of nature or another world.

Fairies are the most fanciful and daintily developed in England.[10] Yeats and the Celtic Revival gentrified, idealized, and pacified the fairies much as Kenneth Grahame gentrified rats and moles. Tolkien referred to hobbits as the "little people". They were very good Good People, being post Yeats and post Grahame. Closer to their Celtic roots, fairies are less refined, and their "pranks" are less amusing. Like Tolkien's Beorn, they are from a merciless time before they were called fairies or put into tales, and our world has shown them little mercy. Fire is a common remedy against them. There is something very primitive, a hint of burnt-offering, in this. The threat of burning was said to chase a changling child and bring the real baby back.[11] Deformed babies were sometimes thrown into the fire, either in a sincere belief that the real child was waiting to appear or because its deformity made it too much of a burden.

After the Cleary case, English courts declared that those engaged in Fairie practices were not continuing old traditions or using them to perpetrate crime but, rather, were insane.[12] What is sanity? What, for that matter, is reality? We see what our physical senses and our experience lead us to believe. If the Cooper's Wife had gone missing in 1995 instead of 1895, her husband would have said she was abducted by aliens, not that she had gone off with the fairies. The difference between little men in green and little green men is a culturally conditioned difference in perception.

Although it continued in the gentrified and socially acceptable Celtic Revival and in the popular imagination, officially, the Cleary case was the beginning of the end of Fairie in Ireland. Slievenamon was a mountain steeped in rebellion as well as Fairie lore. Local peasants imagined the mountain as a ship bound across the sea to Tir na n'Og, the land of eternal youth, the land of heart's desire. It might have been the ship that would bear Tolkien's elves to the West from this world that they were losing. Cracks where heather bloomed on rocky promontories were seen as passageways for other-worldly beings passing to and from the sea. On still, dark evenings, fairy music was heard.[13] People went "out the mountain" to learn Fairie lore or gain aid from those who knew it. However, rebels organized and hid there, making it very much a place of this world. It is ironic that something that happened in the shadow of Slievenamon delayed self-government for Ireland. Rebels and politicians would make a special effort after the Cleary case to eschew the old ways and show how modern and sophisticated Ireland can be.

The southern counties of Ireland eventually gained separate-state status as a republic rather than home rule. In *Meeting the Other Crowd* Lenihan and Greene say that fairy sightings were greatly reduced when electrification came to rural Ireland in the 1950's,[14] the old Ireland died in the 1980's,[15] and intimate Ireland has all but passed away.[16] THEY are still there though in the shadows or driven farther underground beneath the door in the hill, the one that is hidden by that grove of trees and looks very like the doors to Mole End and Bag End. Call them fairies, aliens, hobbits, or Riverbankers, they are always with us or, at least, not far away.

In other parts of the world, especially the United States,[17] the Cleary publicity popularized Fairie, witchcraft, and other forms of the earth religion of the god Pan. In *The Cooper's Wife Is Missing*, published in 2000, Hoff and Yeates speculate that Fairie revivals occur in times of rapid change, such as the late 19th and late 20th centuries.[18] It can also be argued that the more advanced our technology, the greater our need to get back to or down to earth, to literally get into the earth with the fairies, the hobbits, and the Riverbankers. The greater our "knowledge", the greater our need to get back to mystery, fantasy, the unknown. Hoff and Yeates cite the success of the late 20th century films *Photographing Fairies* and *The Blair Witch Project*. I'm sure they would add the early 21st century *Lord of the Rings* films. As he is a writer who never fell into eclipse, it is probably not accurate to refer to a surge in Tolkien's popularity as a Tolkien revival. That Grahame's *The Wind in the Willows* has been loved by all ages for over a century does not signify a revival either but is evidence that the "Little People" are always part of our lives.

The Wide World

"Beyond the Wild Wood comes the Wide World," said the Rat. "And that's something that doesn't matter, either to you or me. I've never been there, and I'm never going, nor you either, if you've got any sense at all. Don't ever refer to it again, please."[1]

Had the Cleary's gone to Clonmel in more prosperous times and been able to support themselves there financially, they probably would have passed their lives largely unnoticed and would never have been world news. They would have been swallowed by the wide world rather than the fairies. Had they never gone to Clonmel at all, they might have lived out quiet, rural lives with little notice from neighbors or fairies. The countryside would have had no need to reclaim them with such violence. It was the conflict of cultures and of the lure of the future and the hold of the past within themselves that turned attention into spectacle and turned illness, suspicion, and discontent into disaster. Bridget and Michael stood out in the insular world of the countryside to which they returned but no longer truly belonged. Living with Bridget's parents, they were exposed again to the fairy beliefs on which they had been raised. In times of crisis, people often return to their earliest beliefs and see them as truths that always were. They are so deeply rooted in the subconscious that there is no conscious memory of learning them. When Tolkien brought his friend C.S. Lewis back to Christianity, Lewis gravitated to the Protestantism of his childhood, not to Tolkien's Catholicism. People find faith in the face of death as a passport not only to heaven but also to a comfort and security known in childhood and exaggerated by memory, an Eden never seen. It is the hope of this Land of Eternal Youth that is inborn and real. Especially in times of trouble, people often return to their roots.

There may be many mansions. Reality may have many layers. There may even be a place where toads drive motorcars and a world inhabited by hobbits with furry feet. Fantasy has many layers of truth. The Cleary case shows that truth is stranger than fiction. It questions where fantasy and truth begin and end. Reality may be a crutch as protest buttons of the 1960's and 1970's said. It may also be a protection. In *His Dark Materials* trilogy, Philip Pullman created a seemingly endless array of worlds and the possibility of moving among them. He concludes, however, that the soul can only survive in its own world. As Tolkien put it, "The tree grows best in the land of its sires".[2]

There have always been insular pockets where people live largely isolated from the realities of the wide world in general and the cultures of which they are part. It would seem to be more difficult to maintain this isolation in the early 21st century than it was in the south riding of County Tipperary in 1895. One can turn off his cell phone and not turn on the 24/7 all-news channels or refuse to own a cell phone or television, but nearly the whole world is better informed of events in the "wide world" than 100 years ago. However, with the loss of community and the popularity of home-schooling and distance-learning, it is probably still possible to live in one's own world. The internet, which can bring the world together at the strike of "enter", actually enables people to establish their own insular community in cyberspace regardless of where they live, and there are people who live their "real lives" in cyberspace. Of course, most people who find their true homes in cyber-communities live full lives in the wide world as well. It has always been true that many people inhabit more than one world and live in more than one reality. Kenneth Grahame and J.R.R. Tolkien were especially adapt at this. "Do we walk in legend or on the green earth of daylight? A man can do both," said Aragorn.[3]

Wind in the Willows depicts a world that is completely fantasized on one level. On another level, it satirized the very "real" world in which Grahame lived. Peter Hunt found another level of reality in the book. The animals live comfortable but limited lives. They do not achieve their ultimate dreams, the important thing being that they *do* yearn, they *do* dream, they *do* sing. "Is that not a form of reality: telling children the truth?"[4] We might have wished Grahame to accept life's limitations for his son.

Of course, Grahame did not achieve his own ultimate dream, which would have been to teach at Oxford as Tolkien later did. No doubt, Grahame would have had a positive impact on his students and thus the world, but anything he might have done as a professor could hardly have had a more positive influence than *Wind in the Willows*, a book that might have died unpublished and never seen the light of the wide world's day.

In his 1919 essay "A Household Book", A.A. Milne wrote: "The books you have read are *The Golden Years* and *Dream Days*.—But the book you have not read—my book—is *The Wind in the Willows*."[5] *The Wind in the Willows* had been one of my favorite books for many years before I even knew that Grahame had written books called

The Golden Years and *Dream Days*. They are not among my favorite books. They differ too much from *Wind in the Willows*. They are not what I would have expected from Grahame, just as *The Wind in the Willows* was too different and not what many who loved his earlier work had expected.

Theodore Roosevelt, like Grahame a committed naturalist and conservationist, was among those who had admired Grahame's earlier work and was at first disappointed in *The Wind in the Willows*. His family loved it and kept at him until he "saw the light" and was converted. He then sang its praises with a convert's zeal.

Roosevelt had asked Grahame for autographed copies of the two earlier works and invited him several times to visit him at the White House. Grahame never went for the White House visit but he did send Roosevelt a manuscript copy of *The Wind in the Willows*. The President told Charles Scribner that it was so wonderful that he must publish it when other publishers in both England and America had turned it down as something that would never sell and Scribner was about to do the same.

Although Grahame never went to the White House to visit Roosevelt, they did meet. They had a long talk after a lecture Roosevelt gave at Oxford in 1910. The then ex-President told the *Saturday Evening Post* that Grahame was simply charming.[6]

In "A Household Book", Milne had said that *The Wind in the Willows* should be a classic, though it had hardly been given time to become one. By a "household book" he did not mean that every household had a copy but that it was a book for everyone in the house, although each person would think it was written just for him. Milne helped to make it a classic and a household book in the first sense by recommending it to everyone he met and by his 1930 play, *Toad of Toad Hall*.

Grahame had rather wanted to see *The Wind in the Willows* as a play. The characters were as real as anyone to him. Why couldn't they appear on stage? Milne saw The Wind in the Willows as a book for all ages as well as "the ages," but he consciously wrote a children's play, to which Grahame readily agreed. The play did much to popularize the book but also to strengthen the popular perception of it as a book for children.

Milne and Roosevelt are admittedly questionable advocate for the importance of *The Wind in the Willows* to adult literature. Milne, of course, wrote the *Winnie the Pooh* series. Near the end of the 20th century much was being made of "the wisdom of Pooh." Pooh would be the first to admit that he's "a silly (if wise) old bear," and they do seem to be stories meant for children, just as *Toad of Toad Hall* is. Pooh, along with *The Wind in the Willows*, owes something to Theodore Roosevelt, as the Teddy Bear was named for him.

Roosevelt spent the entire 60 years of his life in "The Land of Eternal Youth". The British Ambassador stopped by the governor's mansion in April 1900 when Roosevelt was Governor of New York. Edith, Roosevelt's wife, was traveling with her sister at the time, and the ambassador found the governor entertaining the children by lowering them by rope from upper story windows. "You must always remember," the ambassador later wrote, "Roosevelt is about 6".[7]

In 1930, the same year that Milne wrote *Toad of Toad Hall*, E.H. Shepard did illustrations that became very popular for a new edition of *The Wind in the Willows*. He thereby became another person responsible for bringing the Riverbankers and company to the Wide World. Perhaps most people are too tied to the reality of their daily lives to imagine Edwardian rats and moles or toads that drive motorcars unless these characters are clearly drawn on paper and set before their eyes and thus shown to be "real". Shepard himself thought *The Wind in the Willows* was a book that would have been better left without illustrations.

Kenneth Grahame did not really like people and freely admitted it. However, his few close friendships had an important impact on *Wind in the Willows* and its characters. Its popularity in the wide world and the status it achieved as a classic owed nothing to his previous reputation as a writer, which actually hindered its popularity. Its success was due rather to the efforts of a few individuals, most notably Theodore Roosevelt and A.A. Milne and, to a lesser extent, the illustrations of E.H. Shepard and later Arthur Rackham.

Tolkien's works might have become and remained cult classics. Indeed, within the larger interest there is a cult of those who know every character's name and every geographic feature of Middle Earth and even learn to speak the elves' language. However, the 1960's were a time when people prided themselves on being open to old myths and new. Tolkien's books were myths with substance and substance that could be argued and interpreted and endlessly learned. They appealed to students. Many of these students became teachers. They read Tolkien to younger students as children's stories and assigned his work to older students as literature and scholarship. They retained their own interest. Most became parents. They shared Tolkien's stories with their children. There is something in Tolkien, from a final cosmic battle to a hope of peace, that everyone can take away and hold. The *Lord of the Rings* movies of the early 21st century have made Tolkien a favorite of an even wider world.

Academia in general and Oxford in particular are among the somewhat insular societies that exist within the wider world. Perhaps because of its insularity and intellectual inbreeding, Oxford has become a veritable hotbed of modern fantasy in the traditions of Grahame and Tolkien. Grahame had ties to Oxford, but he did not go to the university, and his son did not finish. Yet his tradition is as strong as that of Tolkien, who was a professor there. Richard Adams, who studied history at Oxford, wrote animal fantasy, although it is perhaps more in the realistic tradition of Felix Salten than of Grahame. Philip Pullman went to Oxford University and lives in the town. Oxford is the primary setting of the trilogy *His Dark Materials*, which has similarities to both Tolkien and Grahame.

Like his friend Tolkien, C.S. Lewis was also an Oxford professor. He and Tolkien shared much of the same knowledge and had many of the same interests. They both read the old Norse legends. Lewis's still popular *Chronicles of Narnia* are obviously children's books. Why? What relegates a book to children's literature?

It is not really subject. Children's books often contain violence, loss, sadness, fear, horror, and gruesome death. Their purpose often seems to be to warn, frighten, indoctrinate, and socialize children into the wide world rather than protect them from it. The only taboo subject in children's books has traditionally been sex, and this has been changing, especially in the "young adult" field.

Children identify more easily with young people and animals and are not likely to appreciate a book in which all the characters are adult. However, adults love to have the half-forgotten perceptions of childhood brought back to them. Some stories seen through the eyes of children are not written as children's books at all. Harper Lee's *To Kill A Mocking Bird* is one example. Grahame's *The Golden Years* and *Dream Days* are two others. Kaiser Wilhelm had two books in the cabin of his royal yacht: the Bible and *The Golden Years*.[8]

A circular plot is often considered to be a distinguishing feature of a children's story. The protagonist leaves home, has an adventure, returns to find everything as it had been, and goes on with his life as it was. This theory contends that in adult fiction the characters develop and the plot moves forward in a straight line. "You can't go home again." Would a story in which a man or woman goes off and has a lurid affair, leaves or loses the lover a year later, returns home with the excuse of having had amnesia, finds the family much as it had been, is accepted back, and continues with life as he would have without the interruption be a children's book? Toad returns home but does not find things unchanged. Mole returns to his little house but leaves again and continues with his new life. *The Hobbit*, which can be enjoyed by adults but was written primarily as a children's story, suggests a circular plot in its sub-title: *There and Back Again*. Frodo also returns home in *Lord of the Rings*, but home is not the same. Frodo and his life would not be the same again either.

Vocabulary is not a good indicator that a book is for children either. Most of the best books for children use "big words". Grahame and Tolkien certainly do. Children usually learn more vocabulary through reading than through memorizing lists of words.

I question the practice of dividing literature according to the age of potential readers. Anyone of any age should feel comfortable reading any book that he understands and enjoys and that has meaning for him. However, if there is a legitimate indicator of children's literature, it is tone, the voice in which the writer communicates. Although it has heroes, monsters, and a dragon, John Gardner's *Grendel* is never considered a children's book. This is because of its philosophical concepts and its tone. *The Chronicles of Narnia*, a very good and much loved children's series, are obviously consciously written for children. The tone is controlling and paternalistic[9], and Lewis stopped to explain things that an adult would be expected to know. An adult will probably feel that Lewis is talking down to him, a condescension that is not present in *The Hobbit*. However, the tone of *The Hobbit* is closer to that which would be used in talking to a child than Tolkien would later use in *The Lord of the Rings*. The beginning of *The Wind in the Willows* also has the tone an adult might use in talking to a child. This tone is probably because Grahame and Tolkien started these stories by telling them to their young sons. However, they soon found they were telling and writing the stories for themselves and lapsed into a tone they would use with adults. It is this absence of condesension that makes them everyone's stories and household books.

In a 1967 interview that appeared in *The Sunday Times Magazine* in London and also in *The New York Times Magazine*, Tolkien said that he had come to consider *The Hobbit* to be written in bad style, as if written for children. His children hated anything that marked a book as being for children rather than just people and, when he thought about it, he instinctively did, too. He believed that children are not a separate class but humans at different stages of maturity. As they are not a separate class, they should not have a separate class of literature.

Although he made more distinction in his writing for children and adults, C.S. Lewis himself said that arrested development does not consist in refusing to lose old things but rather in failing to add new.[11] Tolkien contended that what are called fairy stories are as suitable for adults as for children and that only some of each have a taste for them. He believed that, when the taste is innate, it increases rather than decreases with age.[12] In an early review of *The Hobbit*, which Douglas A. Anderson calls a world-wide classic for all ages and all times,[13] Lewis said it should be read and re-read throughout life.[14] A.A. Milne had said much the same for *The Wind in the Willows*.

One can add new interests and new favorite books without discarding the old. It is possible to widen one's world and still conserve the past.

A Death at Oxford

A quarter century after Bridget Cleary died of a chill and an overdose of Fairie lore, another death occurred in which fantasy may have been a contributing factor. Kenneth and Elspeth Grahame's only child died at Oxford University. He was just short of his twentieth birthday and had recently passed his first year exams. He had taken them orally, as he was blind in one eye and had impaired vision in the other. These defects, present from birth, hardly made him a born scholar, although he was apparently quite intelligent. Judging from his pictures, Alastair was a beautiful child and a nice looking young man, although a serious case of acne, which does not show in pictures, attacked him in his teens and remained with him until his death. This made him more self-conscious and shy and socially gauche than he was by nature. His father was also a loner at heart, but Kenneth Grahame was a charming man and could be congenial and convivial when the situation called for it. While his father was quiet and pleasant, Alastair was quiet and taciturn and aloof. He had no social graces, no ability to make small talk, and no ability to quietly "fit in".

Apart from their reputed distaste for sex, Kenneth was 40 and Elspeth in her late 30's when they married. In middle age, they would not have been fonts of fertility and probably did well to produce one child. As the only child of comfortably well-off parents, he was the "little prince" for his first fourteen years. As Elspeth's hopes for Kenneth faded, she pinned them on poor Alastair, who was even less fit to bear the burden. He was the prince of her fantasy world, the most perfect son possible: the most brilliant, the most capable, the most accomplished, the most popular. In her need to monopolize his affections, she seems to have turned him against his father at some point, although father and son might have become estranged on their own. By his late teens, he had tired of her smothering and had drawn away from her as well. "There was no one to whom he could turn."[1]

Although Alastair was the over-protected center of the Grahame household and had "all the advantages", he had to enter his parents' separate fantasy worlds to fully gain their attention. We know that his father spent time with him. After he left the Bank of England, he took Alastair with him on country and woodland walks to share his interest in and love of nature. We don't know if the younger Grahame could communicate with the animals as the elder did or not. Of course, Grahame originally created the talking Riverbank animals for Alastair, which may have been a mixed blessing. A.A. Milne's son was embarrassed by the Pooh stories and resented being Christopher Robin. When Alastair was thrown from the protected world of which he was the center, the world of the Riverbank, into the merciless world of preparatory school, being friends with a rat and a mole could have made the transition even more difficult than was made inevitable by his physical problems and personality. He was not a person who could move among worlds easily as his father could.

We cannot know how Alastair finally felt about *The Wind in the Willows* or his part in its conception. Perhaps he was taunted about it and wished that it would be forgot or had never come to be. He seems to have retained a joking affection for it. A friend wrote him on Palm Sunday 1820 that he was not surprised that he had passed his exams, as they had both determined it should be so if only for the Toad's sake.[2] Might "the Toad" have referred to his father? He must have wished his father had not conceived him either. Perhaps he wanted nothing more than to return to the Riverbank, "The Land of Heart's Desire", and never have to leave again.

Sending Alastair to prep school was comparable to sending Toad to jail. Individual adults tried to be kind, but he was unable to adjust to the system or the society of adolescent boys. Although he was good at the solitary endeavors of swimming and horseback riding, he was physically as well as socially awkward and was useless at the team sports so important to such schools. His acne and squint and academic problems caused by his blindness did not make life any easier. He lasted six weeks at the rough-and-tumble Rugby and over a year at the somewhat less rigid Eton. He had an emotional collapse if not a full-scale nervous breakdown after each attempt. He then studied with private tutors until going to Oxford in 1918.

We have to doubt that Kenneth Grahame shared his wife's idealized image of Alastair. He must have known he still was and always had been as much the Toad as the Prince. However, he must have shared Elspeth's determination that he go to Oxford as Grahame had so very much wanted to do. He could not imagine that Oxford would not be anyone's "Land of Heart's Desire". He could not see that what would have been a joy and a challenge for him would be an unbearable burden for Alastair. He underestimated his son's unsuitability for the academic life. Grahame did tend to retreat into fantasy when life was less than utopian, leaving the crises of this world unattended. Grahame spoke of his dream-city in a speech to the Keats-Shelley Association, a speech that was later reprinted in *Fortnightly Review*. It ended by saying, "—it is by seeing things as better than they are that one arrives at making them better".[3] In Alastair's case, this was not true.

The Grahames had doted on their son, but he was starved for real attention. As a child, he would lie dreamily in the middle of the road as a car approached to get his nurse's attention.[4] At least Peter Green believes that was his reason. Alastair was a mystical child, and his mysticism took a more conventional turn than his father's. He told his governess, Miss Scott, that a picture of Jesus was his friend the Carpenter, who had visited him when he had peritonitis in 1904. He said he sometimes went to talk with the Carpenter. He probably got more practical conversation out of the Carpenter than either of his parents. He also told Miss Scott that death was a promotion.[5] Perhaps he wanted to go stay with the Carpenter.

While under the stress of studying for his exams at Oxford, Alastair was also having a crisis of faith and confessed to being an agnostic. This is hardly unusual for a young university student forced to consider new and contradictory ideas. It must have been particularly difficult for Alastair when added to his other problems. His father knew he could not help with conventional religion. He asked a cleric friend of the family to write to him. He sent him a Concordance, which was undoubtedly not at all what was needed, along with a letter admonishing him to settle in and work hard at Oxford, as he would have a lot to do in a short time. Alastair knew this. Passing his exams gave him more time to worry about religion and his hard years ahead as a scholar.

On May 20, 1920, Alastair asked for a glass of port after dinner, which was not his custom. Did he know it was his last supper? In the early evening, he set out alone across Port Meadow. The name of the wine and the meadow may be coincidence or symbolic of the last of the wine. His pockets were full of religious tracts. His body, clearly decapitated by a train, was found in the early morning by a railway gang on the tracks that crossed the meadow. A coroner's jury convened on May 13 and declared it an accidental death. It *was* Oxford, and several dons were on the jury. It *was* the Grahames. Alastair must have had his blind eye toward the train. He *was* often distracted. He *had* had a glass of port. It may have been dark, or perhaps that dusky, twilight time when one can often see fairies but not the solid things of this world. Alastair *was* always a little fey.

Peter Green says that the testimony of the medical examiner makes it a virtual certainty that Alastair intended to die. "The nature of the injuries makes it almost certain that Alastair lay down across the track, in a slightly diagonal position, his neck and shoulder resting on one rail, his right foot and left leg on the other"[6] (and waited for the train). It does seem that a person walking and hit by a train would be thrown away from the tracks. I would need graphs showing the body being thrown to understand the physical laws of motion involved. For me, the proof of suicide is in Green's question, "Even taking Alastair's blind eye into account, are we to assume that he was also deaf?"[7] A steam engine is a large and loud and very solid object.

His pockets were full of religious tracts. Did he hope that they and the Carpenter would save him as his nurse had done? Was he giving faith a last chance, or did he want to be in Heaven with the Carpenter and think the tracts would serve as his ticket?

Did Alastair know he could never meet his parents' expectations, and had he always wanted their unconditional approval? Did he die to spite them? Kenneth Grahame hated trains. Now a train had taken his son.

Did he die for his parents' fantasies or his own?

The answer may be "all of the above".

Kenneth and Elspeth went to Italy soon after Alastair died. They sold their house and many of the possessions that reminded them of him. They came home and lived their separate eccentric lives. Grahame spent much of his time in his study. Elspeth spent hers bargaining with merchants. They dined together. They drank a lot of wine, but, as Grahame had said years earlier in *A Funeral*, "the grapes are sour, and the hopes are dead".[8]

I had always half wanted to know how Alastair Grahame had died. Along with the question I must have carried a premonition that I wouldn't want to know. The flaps of book covers always state that the stories were originally for him and that he died tragically in 1920 at the age of nineteen. 1920 was too late for World War I, and it would be openly said if he had died in battle. It would be said if he had died of natural causes. I decided that he must have taken up Toad's motorcar mania. That might not be said for fear of dampening the fun of Toad's exploits. I thought that was an ironic and good explanation and didn't try to check on its truth.

After looking up another author in a reference book of children's literature, I decided to see what it said about Grahame. It hit me like the Si Gaoith, like the train hit Alastair. I was in shock. I was devastated that the stories that have brought so much comfort and joy to children and people of all ages and have meant so much to me for so long could not save the child for whom they were created.

I mourned for Alastair, but I mourned more for his father. I don't believe he ever thought it was an accident. If not guilt, regret must have been with him for the rest of his life. He was never close to Elspeth. He was estranged from his relatives. He was too proper and stoic to confide his grief to friends. I could see him alone, saying, "Oh, Ratty. Oh, Mole." It was to them he would have turned.

When E.H. Shepard came to see him in 1930 about illustrating *Wind in the Willows*, Grahame said, "I love these *little people* (my emphasis). Be kind to them".[9]

Although a perfect living child, the idealized Alastair his parents wanted, did not take the defective changling's place; I believe he went with the fairies to Tir na n'Og, with Tolkien's elves to the West, with the Carpenter to Heaven, with the Riverbankers to Pan's island in the River. They are the same place after all. The only illustration in the first edition of *Wind in the Willows* is Graham Robertson's frontispiece titled, "And a River Went out from Eden". Alastair, by being, could be considered as responsible for the book as his father. It probably would not have been written had he not been. What more can we ask of a near-blind boy in a short, sad life of not quite twenty years. As for eternity, I hope that, like the Princess in Yeats' play, he is in "The Land of Heart's Desire" whatever he conceived it to be, dancing, as he never learned to do in life.

II

Beyond

My first reaction when I heard that William Horwood had written a sequel to Grahame's book was delight that I could share new adventures with the Riverbankers. I had mixed feelings only later when I thought about it. I do think Grahame intended the Riverbank to be a place apart from time, a Land of Eternal Youth, and did not intend the animals to age or die. However, Horwood captures Grahame's style and spirit so well that it is difficult to disapprove of the books.

Horwood lives near the banks of the Thames just outside of Oxford and is thus geographically well-placed to continue Grahame's story. The third in the series, *The Willows and Beyond*, in which Rat and Mole pass on to Pan's island in the River, is moving and quite beautiful.

Horwood has said that he didn't consider the ethics of continuing the story and was inspired to do so by E.H. Shephard's print of Mole venturing into the woods alone to look for Badger's house. He knew from Grahame's story where Mole was going but became haunted by the idea that Mole might be headed for a different adventure. As Grahame made his characters so real that they have lives of their own, it can be argued that they have the right to continue with these lives. That Horwood would have a print of Mole and be inspired by it is not surprising. He had previously written a whole series of very long books that are not obviously intended for children about moles living in the shadow of a standing stone in Duncton Wood.

In Jan Needle's 1981 book *Wild Wood*, the Wild Wooders are no more wild than the Riverbankers. The Wild Wooders themselves consider their woods a dark, dank, and dreary place. They don't live there because it's a congenial environment but because they can't afford the more desirable River Bank. They are the working class. They are the servants that Grahame chose to ignore because they weren't essential to his story. In *Wild Wood*, they are tired of being ignored and expendable. The taking of Toad Hall is an act of social revolution, not of wild animals moving into the absent Toad's house.

Boddington Stoat, a serious reformer and outside agitator, moved from across the river just when a hard winter and hard economic times made the Wild Wood ripe for revolution. The book's satire is aimed more at society and revolution than at Grahame's book. As in *Wind in the Willows*, none of the characters are evil. However, self-interest drives their actions and distorts their view of the world. Boddington seems to be a sincere if professional revolutionary, but, either from the extreme nature of his beliefs or consciously as a means to his end, he twists quite innocent events.

Riverbankers simply did not venture into the Wild Wood alone without a good reason. Mole's terrors in the woods were not caused by his imagination or the falling dark or the nature of the forest but by young stoats set on frightening him. There was much sympathy for Mole and anger at the stoats among the general population of the Wild Wood. Mole was not really a Riverbanker but a field animal and did not understand that he was invading the Wild Wooders territory. He was also resented, however, as a Riverbank hanger-on.

Rat was resented more as a useless fellow who spouted poetry and messed about with boats. Badger was considered a traitor to the Wild Wooders, as he had always lived there and had once had to work. Now he associated with Riverbankers when he associated with anyone at all.

Boddington saw a conspiracy against the working class when Rat followed Mole into the woods and they went together to Badger's house, where Otter joined them next day. This was reported by the two young hedgehogs who got lost in the snow on their way to school. They were taken in, treated kindly, and given a breakfast of porridge. It was resented, however, that they were put to cooking a better breakfast of bacon, sausage, toast, and eggs for the Riverbank animals and sent on their way (with a coin it is true) so that a secret meeting could be held. Because of his position, Toad had to be the main focus of the revolution, and he was not even there.

There was no conspiracy against the Wild Wooders, only selfishness, thoughtlessness, and insensitivity. However, much that happened naturally or accidentally in *The Wind in the Willows* is seen as part of the conspiracy against the Riverbank in *Wild Wood*. The army and the military planning and training were hardly necessary in taking Toad Hall. Only Badger and Mole were there. The servants had been thoughtlessly dismissed by Toad's friends. Their services were considered a needless expense with the master of the house away in jail. Baxter Ferret, the narrator of the story and Toad's driver and mechanic, had become serious about the revolution when these friends had dismissed him when he tried to deliver a new car to Toad, whom they had forcibly restrained and put under house arrest at this same time. Needle points out, and Grahame may have agreed, that Badger, Rat, and Mole were thinking of their own reputations and largess from Toad's wealth, and not their "friend" Toad, and certainly not the newly unemployed ferret. Toad escaped from house arrest only to land in the remotest, stoutest, best-guarded prison in England, from which he would return to retake Toad Hall with his friends.

No one seemed especially sorry when Toad Hall was retaken and Boddington Stoat moved on to organize industrial workers. The Wild Wooders were given improved terms of employment and could therefore feel the cause was not entirely lost. The Chief Weasel may have betrayed the revolution. He had become very like Toad while occupying Toad Hall, rather as the pigs who took over George Orwell's *Animal Farm* became like humans. He found managing an army and an estate difficult and expensive. He may have negotiated with the Riverbankers, with whom he had said he always got along, to trade that role for a summer home on the Riverbank and invitations to balls and banquets there. In Horwood's *The Willows and Beyond*, the Riverbankers themselves lead a revolution.

Although a Riverbanker at heart, Kenneth Grahame would have understood the revolution and sympathized with the Wild Wooders. Like a mole, he had tunneled underground on the subway to work at the Bank of England, work that he did not find congenial. He had done volunteer social work in East End London. He was interested in social utopia, such as expressed by writers such as William Morris, if not in social revolution. Grahame rarely mentioned servants, as everyone would be a Riverbanker in his best of worlds. Everyone would have a summer home on the Riverbank at the very least.

Wild Wood is not a children's book, and it is not an easy book to find in the United States. Perhaps that is because *The Wind in the Willows* was quite solidly classified as children's literature by 1981.

Brian Jacques claims influence from Grahame for his *Redwall* series, that does seem to be primarily written for children. Grahame's influence is obvious in his Woodlanders of Mossflower Wood who built medieval Redwall Abbey as a peaceable haven against such vermin as foxes, rats, stoats, and weasels. He probably assumes that Grahame's Ratty, who is certainly not vermin, is not a rat at all but a vole.

Stephen King's popular novels are generally classified as horror stories but have elements of fantasy. He writes primarily for adults but is very good at remembering how it feels to be a child, especially childhood fears. Tolkien's fantasy has elements of horror. Both writers use giant spiders as frightening things of this world made supernaturally large. King's book *It* is a Tolkien adventure set in modern times. IT is a shape-shifter but is a giant spider in the end. The monster to whom Gollum betrays Frodo and Sam is also a giant spider, and Tolkien uses giant spiders in *The Hobbit* as well. King used the concept of other worlds in *Hearts in Atlantis*, one of his books most firmly set in this world. He shares with Tolkien the imagery of the Dark Tower, and his book *The Stand* concerns the final battle between good and evil that some see in *Lord of the Rings*. Gollum, and also Hrothgar's bane Grendel, would be at home in King's books.

To Grendel, the poetic, heroic legends that inspire men are lies.[1] Hrothgar's man Unferth speaks for honor and the heroic ideal. "You think me deluded. Tricked by my own waking fairy tale.—Except in the life of a hero, the whole world's meaningless. The hero sees values beyond what's possible.—It kills him ultimately. But it makes the whole struggle of humanity worthwhile."[2]

Grendel was right, of course. Legends are selective, slanted, and exaggerated, and so is history. He is not completely right however. Opposing sides will have different heroes and legends and will tell history differently but with some truth. There are many layers of truth. Even Grendel wanted to believe in the "projected possible"[3] and was moved by the Shaper's songs. John Gardner mentions middle-earth[4] in *Grendel*. Apparently it was a setting often used in legend.

If legends have some truth and Tolkien was working back through language to re-create lost tales, some aspects of the people who used these languages and their world must once have been. Perhaps Tolkien's stories are as true as those that moved and angered Grendel, as those that Grendel called lies. Tolkien, too, was projecting the possible.

Tolkien's continued popularity has contributed to a proliferation of other wizards and other worlds. I have chosen to let Tolkien represent the kind of fantasy that he wrote. To compare all of the popular series of the same sort that came after him with Tolkien's work would be a separate study in itself, and I have not included them here. I have not included Tolkien's *Silmarillion* in this survey of modern fantasy, as it has never been unfairly classified as a children's book.

The only wizard other than Gandalf with whom I have much familiarity is King Arthur's advisor Merlin. (Harry Potter, of course, is a wizard in training.) The Anglo-Saxons had written down the Scandinavian saga Beowulf but not that of the legendary king of the land they had conquered. *The Matter of Britain, The Arthurian Cycle*, was recorded by the French after the Norman conquest of England as a series of romances. By the time the Englishman Sir Thomas Malory condensed and organized these romances as *Morte D'Arthur* about 1469, the setting had moved to the high Middle Ages. Malory's Arthur, the king we know from *Camelot*, is more like Henry II than the Romanized Celtic warlord who may never have been called king but must have brought many Britons together and been a light for a time in the 5th Century Dark Ages. The only knight at Malory's Round Table who was a genuine Celt was Sir Gawain, whose story had been written by the Pearl Poet about a hundred years earlier in *Sir Gawain and the Green Knight*.

The 5th Century warlord Arthur would have been more like Hrothgar in *Beowulf* and Thiodolf in *The House of the Wolfings* than like the Arthur we know. We don't know if any threads suggesting a round table (the magic ring again), noble ideas of government, or a complex love story go back to the early legend.

Working from Malory, T.H. White wrote the four books of *The Once and Future King* in the late 1930's and early 1940's. That Arthur is in the tradition of the king of the eternal return can be seen in White's title and also in Malory's *Morte D'Arthur*. His death is as important as his life. He died for his people, and he is coming back.

The popular musical *Camelot* was inspired by and based on White's book. The legend became especially popular in America when the newly-widowed Jacqueline Kennedy said that *Camelot* was the model and inspiration for John Kennedy's Presidency.

T.H. White was a Cambridge graduate, proving that fantasy is not the private preserve of Oxford University. The first three books of *The Once and Future King* had been published separately before being combined with the fourth. The whole has been favorably compared with *Wind in the Willows* and the *Lord of the Rings*. The first book in White's series, *The Sword in the Stone*, is sometimes printed separately, as a children's book. In it Merlin changes the young Arthur into a fish, a hawk, a badger, and, in later editions, an ant and a wild goose so that he can know the world from different perspectives. The shape-shifting and juxtaposition of worlds is further complicated by the fact that the wizard is living backwards in time and introduces information from the future.

Actually, White sent a fifth book to his publisher along with the fourth in 1941. At the time, White meant it to be the last book of *The Once and Future King*. It was rejected because England was involved in World War II in 1941. Both the pacifist and war-enthusiast can find confirmation in Tolkien. *The Book of Merlin* is White's unabashed anti-war statement. There were better reasons to reject it. It is more seriously political and philosophical than the other books. It is also somewhat strident, bitter, and tedious. It does not fit with the spirit of the other four, in which White successfully wove legend, satire, and absurdity into a believable reality that is ever shifting and never ponderous even when dealing with serious themes. It is lighter and less grand than *The Lord of the Rings*.

White must have ultimately agreed that book five would be out of place in *The Once and Future King*. He didn't campaign to have it added later. Arthur being turned into an ant and a wild goose were later added to *The Sword in the Stone*. *The Book of Merlin* was found after his death and published in 1977. It was always sold separately but never as a children's book. Alone, it makes an interesting statement on war and society. White would have agreed with John Gardner's *Grendel* that man is the most ferocious animal. White says that man massacres his own species like a cannibal and invented cruelty to animals.

In *The Book of Merlin*, the wizard calls a council of animals at Badger's house to decide what to do about the war Mordred has forced on the king. Arthur is turned into an ant and a wild goose to see how totalitarian and free societies deal with questions of war and the world. Such shape-shifting is not the adventure it had been when Arthur was a boy. It is rather boring if not disconcerting to the old king on the eve of his death. There is a desperate quality to it.

Badger's house is not all that is reminiscent of *The Wind in the Willows*. The entrance to this badger's house looks like a large *mole* hole. Arthur thought Merlin had been shut up like a *toad* in a hole, but the wizard had been arguing with Badger. The book ends with the theory that Arthur is not in Avalon or on Pan's Island in the River or buried beneath a church. His burial mound is a badger hole. He is still there, discussing war and government and how to arrange society.

Mary Stewart's Arthurian trilogy of the 1970's, *The Crystal Cave*, *The Hollow Hills*, and *The Last Enchantment*, centers on Merlin and takes the legend back to its earlier beginnings, to the Dark Ages legends and history of Cornwall, Brittany, and Wales. Cornwall helped inspire *The Wind in the Willows*. Wales was an early inspiration to Tolkien. Stewart uses the term middle-earth.[5] The cave in the hollow hills where Merlin made his home is very like a hobbit house or the homes of Grahame's animals. King Uther refers to it as "your hole in the ground".[6]

Stewart went back beyond fantasy and romance and looked for the possible "real world" facts on which they might have been based. Merlin had "the sight" but was more engineer than magician. He was named for the falcon, and he was said to be closer to wild things than to men.[7] His spirit may have done the sort of shape-shifting that the daemon or soul of Philip Pullman's heroine Lyra will do in a parallel world in another part of time.

In her 1963 *The Mists of Avalon*, Marion Zimmer Bradley also took Arthur's legend back to its Dark Age beginnings. The story attempts to unite the old religion, which centered at Avalon, with Christianity against the invading Saxons. Avalon can be seen as Pan's Isle in the River. It exists as a parallel world in a dimension deeper in the mists behind Glastonbury Abbey. Merlin was a practitioner of the old earth religion, and Arthur was born into it. Arthur's sword Excalibur is the Sword of Avalon. The old religion accepted Christianity as part of itself. One can have both a father and a mother. Guenevere is a disruptive presence in that she is a Christian who does not accept the old ways.

As well as a king of the eternal return, Arthur may also be another were bear. Like Beowulf, the name Artois means bear.

The More Things Change—

The overlapping worlds of Kenneth Grahame and J.R.R. Tolkien were fading fast as the 19th century became the 20th. Every modernization accelerated change. Both authors expressed disdain for the "brave new world" and its "toys" and a preference for simpler times. However, both men adjusted enough to live and succeed in the changing times and even showed interest in and made use of modern inventions. It is ironic to know that one of the new "toys" showed how dangerous it could be in taking the life of Grahame's only child. It leads one to think of H.D. Thoreau, an earlier denizen of the simpler 19th century, when he wrote that we do not ride on the railroad. It rides upon us.

Neither Grahame nor Tolkien could recognize their too modern worlds here in the 21st century. Unless, of course, they would spend their time in the natural world they both loved. The trees, the rivers, the animals are still here, although it is a major concern of the 21st century that we are destroying them with our civilization. It was Grahame's view that it is our own civilizations that we destroy and that nature is always there, waiting to regain lost ground and take over. The tunnels where Badger lived alone had once been a city.

Cities come and go. The natural world and the animals that inhabit it remain, the alpha and omega.

Perhaps because he preferred to write about and, in doing so, make less well-liked animals attractive, Grahame's characters are dismissive of rabbits. Tolkien's characters eat them. When he is lost in the woods in *The Sword in the Stone*, Arthur also wishes he had a rabbit to eat.

Rabbits found a champion and a voice for their own heroic legends in Richard Adams and his 1972 book *Watership Down*. Adams was certainly familiar with *The Wind in the Willows*. The introductory quote at the beginning of his chapter *The Great River* is Grahame's description of Mole's first impression of The River. As Grahame and Tolkien both had a distaste for trains and motor vehicles, it is also interesting to compare the rabbit's eye view of these modern modes of transportation.

Adams may have been influenced by Tolkien in creating their own myths and legends for his rabbits, tales they loved to gather around their story teller to hear. Adams published a collection of these stories years later in *Tales from Watership Down*. He may also have been influenced by Tolkien's work in his creation of rabbit words. This was not a complex language such as that spoken by Tolkien's elves, and I found Lapine and the language of the hedge row to be distracting. Might Adams in part have been satirizing the language Tolkien had so painstakingly created for the elves?

Like Riverbankers and hobbits, rabbits view the forest as a sinister, frightening place. Like the Riverbankers, they are animals of the countryside, although riverbanks are really too wet for them. Apart from using mostly human speech, the rabbits of Watership Down live as rabbits do in nature. They are not halflings or rabbits as people. In that respect and in the often brutal realism of their lives the rabbits of *Watership Down* are more in the tradition of *Bambi*. As in *Bambi*, the lives of animals in the wild are depicted as hard and often cruel, but only Man is capable of evil. The rabbit Fiver said: "There is terrible evil in the world". Holly replied:

> It comes from men. All other elil (enemies) do what they have to do, and Firth (God) moves them as he moves us. They live on the earth, and they need food. Men will never rest till they've spoiled the earth and destroyed the animals.[1]

Strawberry told General Woundwort and the Efrafa Warren council:

> Animals don't behave like men. If they have to fight, they fight; and if they have to kill, they kill. But they don't sit down and set their wits to work to devise ways of spoiling other creatures' lives and hurting them. They have dignity and animality.[2]

It can be argued that domesticated animals and pets lose a portion of this innocence of evil in emulating the ways of the people with whom they live. And in both *Bambi* and *Watership Down* people sometimes help and even save wild animals and are not completely or irredeemably evil. The attack on Watership Down by the Efrafa rabbits might be compared to Tolkien's great battle, but those under Woundwort's control are misled rather than evil. The same, of course, can also be said of Tolkien's final battle in *Lord of the Rings*. Woundwort himself, who acts more like a man than a rabbit, has vague memories of a gentler life and becomes a dark hero in lapine legend. The Watership Down rabbits even see some advantage in moderate measures of Efrafa's discipline and organization.

The Efrafa Warren was organized into Marks, so called from physical marks inflicted on the rabbits. One wonders if the Germanic geographic term Mark, used by Morris and Tolkien, originally signified the land held by a tribe or group whose members were given a certain physical "mark" to distinguish them from others.

Adam's characters are as memorable and their story as absorbing as in any book "peopled" by humans. The reader cannot refrain from cheering them on, sharing their fears, and worrying over their dangers. *Watership Down* is a heroic story, the sort of which legends are made.

When *Watership Down* was published in 1972, *The Methodist Recorder* wrote: "There are five supremely great writers of books which appeal both to children and adults. The first are familiar: Lewis Caroll, Kenneth Grahame, A.A. Milne, Tolkien, and now . . . . there is Richard Adams". I would add Philip Pullman.

Pullman claims John Milton's *Paradise Lost* as the inspiration and basis for his trilogy *His Dark Materials*, consisting of *The Golden Compass, The Subtle Knife*, and *The Amber Spyglass*. Milton had considered doing the Arthurian cycle as his major work but decided on the Bible and loss of Eden. Pullman was not writing primarily for believers in the Genesis account or to foster belief in the Bible but to create a basis for belief in the mystery and wonder of the universe for children growing up in a world without firm values or unquestioned faith. His universe is vast, many-layered, and mysterious, whether or not one thinks divinity is involved. The mysteries may be fantastic and supernatural or only unexplained. He blends science and technology with fantasy and the magical and mystical in truly creative ways. In the "real world" in which we live the lines between them are often thin. His setting is the place where the string theory of physics meets philosophy and myth through a leap of imagination and faith. He deals with Gardner's "projected possible" outside of time and space.

Pullman credits John Milton, William Blake, and every book he ever read as influences. Surely *Beowulf* and the old Norse tales played some part in inspiring a story that looks to the North. Lyra, the main protagonist, wants to join the expedition to the North. The North promises great adventure and great possibilities. The action is going to happen in the North. Something mysterious is waiting in the North.

There is something of *Beowulf* in Pullman's armored polar bears. Surely Lyra's friend Iorek, like Tolkien's Beorn, is a werebear. He puts on his armor and becomes like a man. Beorn put on his bearskin and became like a bear. Iorek is also similar to Grahame's animals in wearing clothes (armor) and using human speech. He is most reminiscent of the wise Badger.

Whether or not they were intended, there are parallels to Tolkien in Pullman's trilogy. The golden compass is similar to the mirror of Galadriel. The subtle knife is broken and is mended by Iorek. In *Lord of the Rings* Aragorn's sword Auduril is "the sword that was broke". Both Tolkien and Pullman use birds that speak and black clouds of birds.

At first the reader may think Lyra is living in our world. It even has an Oxford, that being where she lives. As subtle differences continue to appear, it becomes obvious that reality has slipped a degree or so. It is a similar but slightly different world. No one is ever alone there. The soul or daemon is mystically attached but external and is carried along in the form of an animal as the perfect pet, friend, companion, other self. It is always available for unspoken advice, comfort, and company. In childhood, before a personality is set, it is constantly changing from one animal form to another. It is the ultimate shape-shifter and the ultimate halfling. Lyra's daemon is Pan (Pantalaimon).

Lyra travels in a seemingly endless array of worlds, but, in the end, they are not for her. Like Grahame's Riverbankers, she learns that life is limited.

Willow, called by his creator, Camilla Ashforth, "the gentlest bear you will ever meet", may not be in the tradition of Beowulf or Arthur or Tolkien's Beorn. However, the Teddy Bear hero of these beautiful books that are undoubtedly meant for children but are a delight to eyes of all ages is reminiscent of Grahame's Ratty in that he lives by the river and loves picnics and "messing about with boats". Willow has an affinity for the ocean and loves to spend time at Salt Cottage, his cottage by the sea. Ratty, of course, had to be physically restrained from going with the Sea Rat to sea. The Wild Wooders of Jan Needle's book *Wild Wood* would be pleased to know that Willow works quite hard feeding all the animals on his farm before setting off for a day on the river. He is a Riverbanker with a very visible means of support. Grahame and Tolkien would be pleased to know that, in an age of technology that they could not have imagined and would not have wished to imagine or use, Willow carries neither a cell phone nor a lap top computer and prefers the simple pleasures of swings and boats and picnics and playing on the beach to video games and computer games and electronic toys. He would rather row down the river with his friend Finley or frolick with Little Pig

Pink than "chat" online. He not only appreciates the simple pleasures but also appreciates sharing them.

As are the works of Grahame and Tolkien on a larger scale, the Willow books are about friendship, responsibility, and trust. They are about the intimacy of life in the natural world, even when the boundaries of that world blur and Teddy Bears take on human roles and attributes as "Bear" sometimes did in legend.

It has not been my purpose to suggest that the 20th century fantasy writers consciously borrowed each other's ideas and images but that there are similarities in their works and that a common tradition has developed in modern fantasy out of earlier traditions of legend and myth. This tradition is timeless and ageless and is not a protected garden for children from which adults should be excluded. It can lead to danger and tragedy in the darkest depths of the Wild Wood. However, it is not a tradition based on darkness. It is based on a preference for peace and on respect for nature and each other and for things that were or might have been as well as those that are and are yet to be.

We tend to see the primeval world as either a garden or a wilderness. The garden has constrictions. The wilderness has dangers. Freedom or security is a basic human choice. Both freedom and security have limits. Choice limits future choice, for the world as well as the individual. The Wild Wooders are only our neighbors. Their lives are limited, too. Down in Badger's tunnels, which were part of a civilization long ago, the wizards, shape-shifters, and eternal kings are still discussing how people can share this world's limited space and resources with each other and the other residents of the earth and whether the Fourth Age, Tolkien's Age of Man, will also end, as Middle Earth did.

Appendix I

THE CLEARY CASE:
A POLITICAL EXPLANATION

Of course, a more worldly if little less fantastic spin can be put on the Cleary Case than those given in *The Dark Side of Fairie*. We know so little about the Clearys that, with one turn of the kaleidoscope, the story can completely change. Bridget and Michael can be seen as very sophisticated for their time and place, although self-serving ambition and self-preservation can be found anywhere and in any time.

Both Clearys were ambitious. They had tried to succeed in the city. They had no qualms about moving into Bridget's parents' government-provided cottage to save money when they could not support themselves there. Bridget did sewing and sold eggs. She was planning to raise pigs. Michael had a shop at home and traveled as an itinerate cooper when not employed in town. Both traveled; Bridget shorter distances delivering, her sewing and eggs. Both were well placed to gather information.

Sleveamon had long been a refuge of rebels. Some of the family and neighbors who used her parents' house as a gathering place may have had such leanings. Bridget was often around, doing "women's work". She would have known things.

Many speculated that Bridget was having an affair with the land agent William Simpson. Might she have been dealing in information instead? Could Bridget Cleary have been a spy? Might she even have been a double agent?

The Clearys seem to have been people who would be more interested in forging a comfortable place for themselves in the world than in who was in charge of the government. Was Bridget tortured to find out what she knew or might have told? This would explain the Simpson's rather odd interest in the proceedings and their failure to try to stop them. It also helps to account for the relatively light sentence given Michael and the fact that many, including jurors, apparently believed that Michael believed his story.

In this version of events, Michael could well have been a spy himself. He had to kill his wife to disassociate himself from her. He had to prove that he fit into her family and the local community, even if she no longer did.

We can turn the kaleidoscope again, but the picture is confused. There were those on both sides, those who wanted a completely independent Ireland and those who wanted to remain completely a part of Britain, who were glad to have Home Rule dead. Were there those on both sides who were glad to have Bridget dead as well?

Most of those involved may have truly believed that Bridget was off with the fairies. It may have been a way of saying she was not really a spy but was simply not herself. It may have been a ploy to show the Irish as not sophisticated enough for Home Rule. It may have been a cover-up for a murder, not by an angry or jealous husband, but a fellow traveler, saving his own neck.

The Cleary's occupy a larger place in history than they likely would have in life. They may exemplify the 20th century, not the past. Were they really without beliefs, scruples, or loyalties? Regardless of her beliefs, motives, or deeds, Bridget was a sacrifice, perhaps to the century to which she was so boldly striding. I see her with the fairies, on a white horse. Perhaps she rides with them still.

> They stole little Bridget
> For seven years long.
> When she came down again,
> Her friends were all gone.
> They took her lightly back,
> Between the night and morrow.
> They thought that she was fast asleep,
> But she was dead with sorrow.

> from "The Fairies"
> by William Allingham
> Irish poet 1824-1889

Appendix II

ROMANCE AND/OR REVOLUTION

Seven years before Bridget Cleary died horribly in South Tip, Ireland, another young Irish woman met a gruesome death in the slums of London, at least so we are told. Mary Jane Kelly is remembered as Jack the Ripper's fifth and final canonical victim. She was born in Castletown in County Limerick, Ireland, in 1863. She accompanied her father to Wales when he went there to work. When she was 16, she married a local collier there, but she was widowed while still in her teens by a mine explosion. She then moved in with a cousin in Cardiff and became a dock-side prostitute. However, life had better plans for Mary Kelly, at least for the short term.

Mary moved to London and worked in a high-class prostitution house in the West End, where, as she told friends, she enjoyed the company of gentlemen, one of whom took her to France. Mary Kelly may have been within touching distance of a life of which Bridget Cleary would not even dream. She saw Paris but did not care for France, although she continued to sometimes affect the name Marie Jeannette. On returning to London, she did not resume her life in the West End. Had she made dangerous enemies? Was she thought to be dangerous herself? Was she dumped in Whitechapel? Did she simply sink into the slums so soon and so young? Were there people there who could watch her? Was she there to watch others? Ever since her days with sailors on the Cardiff docks, she was well positioned to gather information. She very likely knew both British loyalists and Irish rebels. Might she, too, have been a spy or double agent? She may have known she was trapped in a dangerous game. Fears she expressed for her life seemed more specific than the fear of a prostitute when such were being killed in Whitechapel.

The crimes can be seen as meant to send a message. Some see Masonic ritual in the murders. Masonic and Orange lodges were nearly the same thing at that time in Britain. A cut throat is a universal warning for silence, and mutilation is a symbol of degradation. They could have been done by those on either side of the Irish question. If Mary was playing both sides, perhaps she did have loyalty in the end. She expressed a desire to return to Ireland. This may have been more than a desire to escape a situation she could no longer control.

Although she had fallen far, Mary had a better standard of living than many of the East End residents. She had a small room, which she retained in spite of being behind in her rent. Her landlord's name was McCarthy, her mother's maiden name. He was an Irishman and may have been her uncle. Her last boyfriend, Joseph Barnett, was born of Irish immigrants to the East End. He had moved out because Mary would sometimes let prostitutes who could not afford a bed for the night share the room. However, he continued to visit her and gave her money when he could. Joseph Fleming, her boyfriend before Barnett, also sometimes visited her and gave her money, apparently out of friendship. Besides turning tricks, Mary usually had a live-in boyfriend to help with expenses.

Life was often hand to mouth, day-to-day, or night-to-night in Whitechapel in 1888. Day laborers would stand in line most of the night to compete for one day's work. Beds were rented by the night and prostitutes had to earn their "doss" (bed) money and resist spending it for drink. I doubt that it was Mary Kelly who died in room 13, Miller's Court in November 1888. The body was butchered beyond credible recognition, and, even considering the technology available at the time, scant effort was made to identify it. One hopes that Mary did not lure a woman who could not afford a bed that night into her room to die for her. However, it's quite possible that Mary saved herself or that others saved her, at least until they could find out what she knew.

Of course, the killer could have escaped in Mary's clothes, but there were several sightings of her in the vicinity several hours after she was supposedly killed, one with Joseph Barnett. This suggests that she and Joseph did not know that she was officially dead. She was still in town and not in hiding.

The streets were lined for her funeral, although her relatives had been contacted but did not come. Did her relatives not want to bring anyone's wrath down on the family, or did they know she was alive? Near the end of the next century, the more opulent funeral of Princess of Wales Diana would bring such a mass of mourners forth. Mary might have been dead, an old-time sacrifice, princess for the day. Perhaps in her short life Mary Jane Kelly had also become important.

Like fairies, spies are ethereal creatures seeming to vanish into other-worldly realms. However, the links between Bridget Cleary and Mary Kelly are tenuous and speculative. Both were Irish, ambitious, and may have been spies. If the reader is wondering what the Ripper and his presumed final victim are doing in this book, it is a fair question. He must have been flesh and blood as his crimes most gruesomely were. Yet he might have stepped out of the world of Fairie and disappeared back into it for all that's known of who committed these crimes and why.

I'm not a Ripperologist. I have no vested interest in any theory and no candidate to put forth. The stories keep me casually interested because I doubt the case can ever be solved and think it will always be a mystery. Fleet-foot Jack could be so many men. So many stories could be true. As with the Cleary case, it is not so much a puzzle as a kaleidoscope. One small turn and the pieces fall into a completely different and seemingly credible story. Jack could have been a were-wolf or were-bear. He could have been Tolkien's Beorn, the troll under the bridge, or the Minotaur. He could be the shy professional man or aristocrat who liked to slum. He could be the friendly tradesman. He could be the man you never notice on the street.

I was reading about Kenneth Grahame when one of the "final solutions" came out. Through his position at the Bank of England and his East End social work, Grahame met all kinds of people. It occurred to me that he might have met the Ripper. 'With one long mental leap, he might have been the Ripper. No. I'm not serious. But Lewis Carroll has been suggested as a candidate, after all. The Rabbit Hole Ripper. The Riverbank Ripper. Actually, I believe it was Badger. He had all of those underground tunnels in which to work. Some may well have extended to Whitechapel.

Whoever he was, like Grahame's characters and W.B. Yeats' fairies, the Ripper has been gentrified. Like the incredibly cruel Count Dracula, he has also been romanticized. He has entered the Land of Fairie and become myth. Perhaps he was a romantic gentleman, but even as a romantic myth he reminds us of the dark side.

Appendix III

TWILIGHT AT DAWN

To some, the word millennium only means a thousand year cycle on the scale by which time is being measured. To others, it means "Judgment Day": the cataclysmic end of the world that we know and the establishment of "Christ's Kingdom" on earth. There have always been rumors that the world was about to end and cults that have formed around them. But too many people took seriously even if they fell short of certainty and actual belief to be called a cult, and too many factors were involved to call it a rumor in 2000 when the millennium as well as the century was changing. That should open doors through which the world could fall. And apart from the belief of Christians in the "Millennium", the Mayan calendar predicts that the world would end December 21, 2012. This is the winter solstice, an auspious time of endings. And astronomers did say that a meteor would pass dangerously close to the earth around this time, just missing the planet or knocking it out of orbit. This would very effectively end the world without resorting to help from spiritual or occult beliefs.

The turn of the century/millennium was also a time of economic hardship, uncertainty, and stress which only became worse in the early years of the 21st century. People always turn to fantasy for its escapist aspects in such times. But reality had become less believable than any fantasy. What could be more fantastic than cyberspace or string theory? What had been science fiction in the mid-twentieth century had become reality. For many, the world they had known had already ended. With the borders between fantasy and reality blurred it seems natural for the two to co-exist in the turn the genre has taken.

Two series of "young adult" literature, *Harry Potter* and *The Twilight Saga* were very popular as the new century and millennium dawned. I enjoyed reading both series and both raised interesting questions. I did not include them for several reasons. 1) They have not been tested by time. 2) They are not in the nature-based tradition of Tolkien and Grahame.

I do not know the thinking or intentions of the authors of *Harry Potter* and *Twilight* or paths the writing took, but interesting questions arose as I read. *Harry Potter* was intended originally for middle school boys. As Harry matured and as it attracted a wider and more sophisticated and mature readership, the books became more complex and sophisticated and the story more interesting. I wondered if a series was always intended or a response to popularity. Adults discovered and enjoyed it as they read it to their children or wanted to be familiar with what their children were reading. Not all adults who looked at it liked it. A rumor spread that it was about Satan worship, increasing its popularity and curiosity about it. I wondered if it became more sophisticated because its adult readership grew or its adult readership grew because it became more sophisticated. It did attract adults almost from the start. The youth room copy was always checked out with a waiting list at the library where I worked at the turn of the century. People asked me at the reference desk if there wasn't a copy in the adult collection. One man started to leave but turned back and said in a confidential and embarrassed way: "You know; they're good".

Not only are the Harry Potter books not in the nature-based tradition, they have few animal characters. As a good witch should, Hermione has a cat. Harry's mail is delivered by the white owl Hedwig. My only real emotional response to the books was when Hedwig was in danger and died, perhaps in the old tradition of sacrifice to save Harry and his friends.

Harry Potter takes the very old tradition of witches and wizards and weaves it into mundane life in the modern world. Historically, wizardry was a dangerous occupation. Elizabeth I of England had her court wizard to look into the future, but witches and wizards were often burned at the stake. Harry and his friends grow up to produce more witches and wizards and live mundane lives. In this sense it follows the form of children's literature. The story is circular. The adventure ends with everyone safely back home.

The Twilight Saga gentrifies the old and gruesome legends of vampires and werewolves and gives these once-frightening halflings mundane lives in the everyday modern world. Its popularity started as a cult among adolescent and pre-adolescent girls, but my twenty-something cousin and her friends were early followers. My cousin's enthusiasm inspired me to start reading it.

I liked the first book and didn't see why it would be classified as "young adult". The protagonist is very mature and capable at eighteen. There are few hints of the paranormal. The hardest thing to believe was that vampires can hide so successfully in plain sight. I was impressed by the author's use of formal English. I believe that fiction writers who are said to have majored in English and surely must know correct formal use of the language sometimes choose not to use it for fear of appearing to their readers to be better-than-thou "snobs". Having been programmed for correct formal usage informal stands out for me as incorrect. I'm only saying that I notice these things. I assumed that she was probably being careful to be a good influence on her targeted early-teen readers. From there I deduced that this would be a "morality" tale, aimed at showing her young readers the importance of making sensible decisions in their lives. I thought that I was inside Stephenie Meyers' head. I will only tell you that I was wrong.

But might I have guessed her original intentions? Did her intentions change with her readership? The movies made from both *Twilight* and *Harry Potter* increased the popularity of the books. Their greatest legacy may be the enthusiasm for reading that they generated. But the special effects and technical sophistication on the screen may be as responsible as the words on the printed page for the wide appeal of both series. In the case of *Twilight*, the actors who played Edward and Jacob, the vampire and werewolf, attracted not only women of all ages but men who identified with them and wanted to emulate or be them.

I found it especially interesting that Meyers was less careful and precise, less formal, in her use of the language as the series progressed. Was this because of the pressure and time restraints of getting more books out, or was she consciously speaking to an expanded audience of which she was aware. This audience included all ages and both sexes, making a good argument against classifying books by expected readers.

Bibliography

Books

Adams, Richard. *Watership Down*. NY: Avon, © 1972.

Anderson, Douglas A., ed. *Tales Before Tolkien: the Roots of Modern Fantasy*. NY: Ballentine Del Rey Books, 2003.

Ashforth, Camilla. *Willow on the River*. Cambridge, MA: Candlewick Press, 2001.
   Willow by the Sea. Cambridge, MA: Candlewick Press, 2002.

Bourke, Angela. *The Burning of Bridget Cleary*. NY: Viking, 2000.

Bradley, Marion Zimmer. *The Mists of Avalon*. NY: Knopf, 1963.

Carpenter, Humphrey. *Tolkien: A Biography*. Boston: Houghton Mifflin, 1977.

Gardner, John. *Grendel*. NY: Alfred A. Knopf, 1971.

Graham, Eleanor. *Kenneth Grahame*. NY: Henry Z. Walck, 1963.

Grahame, Kenneth. *The Wind in the Willows*. NY: Alfred A. Knopf, 1993. (first published 1908).

Grambo, Rebecca L. *Bear: A Celebration of Power and Beauty*. San Francisco: The Sierra Club, 2000.

Green, Peter. *Beyond The Wild Wood*. NY: Facts on File, 1983.

Green, Peter. *Kenneth Grahame: A Biography.* Cleveland and NY: World Publishing, 1959.

Heaney, Seamus, translataor. *Beowulf.* NY: Farrar, Strauss, Giroux, 2000.

Hoff, Joan and Marian Yeates. *The Cooper's Wife is Missing*. NY: Basic Books, 2000.

Horwood, William. *The Willows in Winter*. NY: St. Martin's, 1993.
    Toad Triumphant. NY: St. Martin's, 1995.
    The Willows and Beyond. NY: St. Martin's, 1998.

Hunt, Peter. *The Wind in the Willows: A Fragmented Arcadia.* Twayne's Masterwork Series, No. 141. NY: Twayne, 1994.

Jakubowski, Maxim and Nathan Braund, eds. *Jack the Ripper*. NJ: Castle Books, 2005.

King, Stephen. *The Girl Who Loved Tom Gordon*. NY: Scribner, 1999.

King, Stephen. *Hearts in Atlantis*. NY: Scribner, 1999.

King, Stephen. *It*. NY: Viking, 1986.

Lenihan, Eddie with Carolyn Eve Green. *Meeting the Other Crowd: The Fairy Stories of Hidden Ireland*. NY: Jeremy P. Tarcher/Putnam, 2003.

Milne, A.A. "A Household Book". *Not That It Matters*. NY: E.P. Dutton, 1926, (first published 1919).

Morris, William. *The House of the Wolfings*. London: George Prior, 1979, (first published 1889).

Needle, Jan. *Wild Wood*. London: Andre Deutsch, 1981.

Porteous, Alexander. *The Forest in Folklore and Mythology*. NY: Dover, 2002, (first published 1928)

Pullman, Philip. *His Dark Materials*.
  The Golden Compass. NY: Alfred A. Knopf, 1995.
  The Subtle Knife. NY: Alfred A. Knopf, 1997.
  The Amber Spyglass. NY: Alfred A. Knopf, 2000.

Salten, Felix. *Bambi*. NY: Grossett and Dunlap, 1929.
  Bambi's Children: NY: Grosset and Dunlap, 1939.

Shippey, T.A. *J.R.R. Tolkien: Author of the Century*. NY: Houghton Mifflin, 2001.

Stewart, Mary. *The Crystal Cave*. NY: William Morrow, 1970.
  The Hollow Hills. NY: William Morrow, 1973.
  The Last Enchantment. NY: William Morrow, 1979.

Tolkien, J.R.R. *The Annotated Hobbit*. Annotated by Douglas A. Anderson. Boston: Houghton Mifflin, rev. and expanded ed., 2002.

Tolkien, J.R.R. *The Hobbit*, Boston: Houghton Mifflin, 1966.

Tolkien, J.R.R. *The Lord of the Rings*. Boston: Houghton Mifflin, 1965.

Tolkien, J.R.R. *Tree & Leaf*. "On Fairy Stories". Boston: Houghton Mifflin, 1989.

White, T. H. *The Book of Merlyn*. Austin and London: University of Texas Press, 1977.

White. T.H. *The Once and Future King*. NYU: Putnam's Sons, 1958.

Wilde, Oscar. *The Happy Prince and Other Fairy Tales*. Minola, NY: Dover, 2001.

Yeats, W.B. "The Land of Heart's Desire". *Great Irish Plays*. Avenel, NJ: Gramercy, 1995.

Media

Lord of the Rings: Beyond the Movie. Kathleen Phelan, writer and producer. *National Geographic Explorer*, 2002.

Tr: An American Lion. The History Channel, 2003.

Web Sites

Jacques, Brian. www. redwall.org online 16 Jan. 2003.

Milne, A.A. www.geocities.com/willowind online 9 Dec. 2002.

Endnotes

Notes for Introduction

1   Jacques, Brian. www.redwall.org. Online 16 Jan. 2003.

2   Tolkien, J.R.R. "On Fairy Stories," Note A, p. 66.

3   Anderson, Douglas A. *Tales Before Tolkien*, p. 430.

4   Milne, A.A. www.geocities.com/willowind. Online 9 Dec. 2002.

5   Tolkien, J.R.R. "On Fairy Stories." Note A, p. 66.

6   Anderson, Douglas A. Note 2, p. 30.

7   Hunt, p. 8.

8   Green, Biography, p. 191.

9   Shippey, p. 154.

10   The Fellowship of the Ring, p. 281.

11   The Two Towers, p. 324.

12   Ibid., p. 269.

13   Ibid., p. 221.

14   The Hobbit, p. 73.

15   The Return of the King, p. 305.

16   Ibid., p. 309.

17   Ibid., p. 177.

18   Grahame, p. 43.

19   Green, Beyond the Wildwood.

20   The Hobbit, p. 240.

21   Hunt, p. 115.

22   Ibid., p. 65-66.

23   Carpenter, p. 201.

24   Anderson, p. 21.

Notes for the Writers and Their World

1. Carpenter, p. 58.
2. Hunt, p. 85.
3. *The Wind In The Willows*, pp. 142-143.
4. Hunt, p. 86.
5. Green, Beyond the Wildwood, p. 118.
6. Carpenter, p. 159.
7. Ibid., p. 216.
8. Ibid., p. 222.
9. Ibid., p. 163.
10. *The Hobbit*, p. 317.
11. Lenihan, p. 330.

Notes for Similarities in the Books

1. The Annotated Hobbit, p. 17.
2. The Fellowship of the Ring, p. 279.
3. Ibid., 126.
4. Ibid., p. 137.
5. Ibid., p. 396.
6. The Two Towers, p. 274.
7. The Hobbit, p. 41.
8. Ibid., p. 101.
9. Ibid., p. 109.
10. Ibid., p. 178.
11. The Wind in the Willows, p. 41.
12. The Two Towers, p. 62.
13. Ibid., p. 46.
14. Ibid., p. 43.
15. Carpenter, p. 162.
16. Ibid.
17. Shippey, pp. 60-61.
18. The Fellowship of the Ring, p. 144.
19. The Two Towers, p. 152.
20. The Fellowship of the Ring, p. 329.
21. Ibid., p. 305.

22   Anderson, Note 2, p. 29.
23   The Hobbit, pp. 80-81.
24   Anderson, Note 10, p. 234.
25   Ibid., p. 97.
26   The Fellowship of the Ring, p. 237.
27   The Return of the King, pp. 291-292.
28   Ibid., p. 265.
29   Ibid.
30   The Wind in the Willows, p. 224.
31   Ibid., p. 230.
32   The Two Towers, p. 150.
33   The Return of the King, p. 285.
34   The Fellowship of the Ring, p. 283.

Notes from the River's Source

1   Green, Beyond the Wild Wood, p. 144.
2   Ibid., p. 160.
3   Ibid., p. 143.
4   Porteous, p. 62.
5   Shippey, p. 31.
6   Grambo, p. 161.
7   Ibid., p. 20.
8   Ibid., pp. 41-42.
9   Ibid. p. 20.
10   Ibid., p. 31.
11   Shippey, p. 32.
12   Ibid.
13   The Two Towers, p. 89.
14   Hoff, p. 79.
15   Ibid., p. 82.
16   Lerihan, p. 279.
17   The Two Towers, p. 310.
18   The Hobbit, p. 11.
19   Carpenter, p. 136.
20   Ibid., p. 220.
21   The Two Towers, p. 252.

22   Anderson, Note 23, p. 219.

23   The Return of the King, p. 279.

Notes for the Wild Wood

1   Morris, p. 155.

2   Carpenter, p. 70.

3   *The Hobbit*, p. 149.

4   Ibid. p. 143.

5   Needle, p. 83.

6   Morris. p. 169.

7   Ibid. p. 37.

8   Ibid. p. 29.

9   Ibid. p. 34.

10   Ibid., p. 27.

11   *Bambi*, p. 234.

12   Ibid., p. 264.

13   *Bambi's Children*, pp. 46-47.

14   *The Two Towers*, p. 77.

15   Porteous, p. 152.

16   Ibid. p. 252.

17   Ibid., p. 51.

18   Ibid., pp. 258-259.

19   Ibid., p. 34.

20   *The Two Towers*, p. 44.

21   Porteous, p. 229.

22   *The Return Of The King*, p. 30.

23   Ibid., p. 87.

24   Ibid., p. 249.

25   *The Two Towers*, p. 155.

26   Porteous, p. 156.

27   *The Two Towers*, p. 155.

28   Porteous, p. 270.

29   *The Fellowship Of The Ring*, p. 141.

30   Ibid.

[31] Porteous, p. 277.

[32] Gardner, p. 130.

[33] Ibid., p. 32.

[34] Ibid., p. 49.

[35] Ibid., p. 11.

[36] Ibid., p. 48.

[37] *The Girl Who Loved Tom Gordon*, p. 107.

[38] Ibid., p. 22.

[39] Ibid., p. 21.

[40] Ibid., p. 60.

[41] Ibid., p. 67.

[42] Ibid., p. 86.

[43] Ibid., p. 9.

[44] Ibid., p. 107.

Notes for the Dark Side of Fairie

[1] Great Irish Plays, p. 592.

[2] The Wind in the Willows, p. 135.

[3] Hoff, p. 72.

[4] Ibid., p. 250.

[5] The Wind in the Willows, p. 124.

[6] Anderson, Note 5, p. 199.

[7] Lenihan, pp. 174-179.

[8] Ibid., p. 276.

[9] Ibid., p. 187.

[10] Porteus, p. 89.

[11] Lenihan, pp. 296 and 298.

[12] Hoff, p. 404.

[13] Ibid., p. 77.

[14] Lenihan, p. 165.

[15] Ibid., p. 2.

[16] Ibid., p. 3.

[17] Hoff, p. 405.

[18] Ibid., p. 392.

Notes for The Wide World

1   The Wind in the Willows, p. 16.
2   The Return of the King, p. 252.
3   The Two Towers, p. 37.
4   Hunt, p. 118.
5   Milne, p. 86.
6   Beyond the Wild Wood, pp. 185-186.
7   TR: An American Lion.
8   Beyond the Wild Wood, p. 177.
9   Hunt, p. 113.
10   Anderson, Note 18, p. 76.
11   Hunt, p. 115.
12   Tree and Leaf, p. 33.
13   Anderson, p. 23.
14   Ibid., p. 18.

Notes for a Death at Oxford

1   Green, Beyond the Wild Wood, p. 202.
2   Ibid., p. 200.
3   Ibid., p. 206.
4   Ibid., p. 138.
5   Ibid., p. 200.
6   Ibid., p. 201.
7   Ibid.
8   Ibid., p. 202.
9   Graham, Eleanor, p. 39.

Notes for Beyond

1   Gardner, p. 49.
2   Ibid., p. 89.
3   Ibid., p. 49.
4   Ibid., p. 32.

5   The Crystal Cave, p. 35.
6   Ibid., p. 443.
7   Ibid., p. 35.

Notes for the More Things Change

1   Adams, p. 163.
2   Ibid., p. 249.